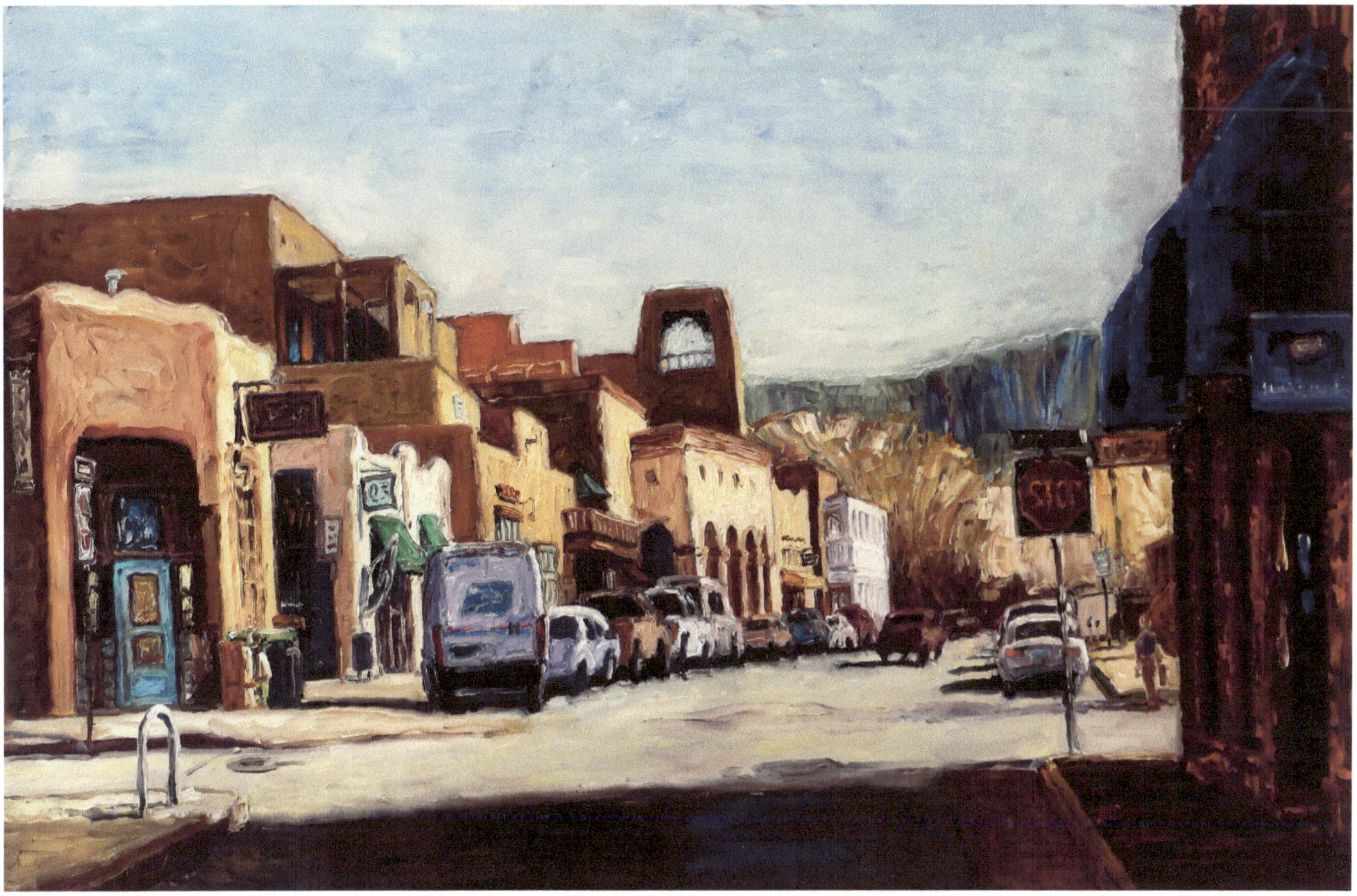

"Street in Santa Fe" 42" x 36" oil on canvas

Expanded views of these two paintings appear on the following pages:

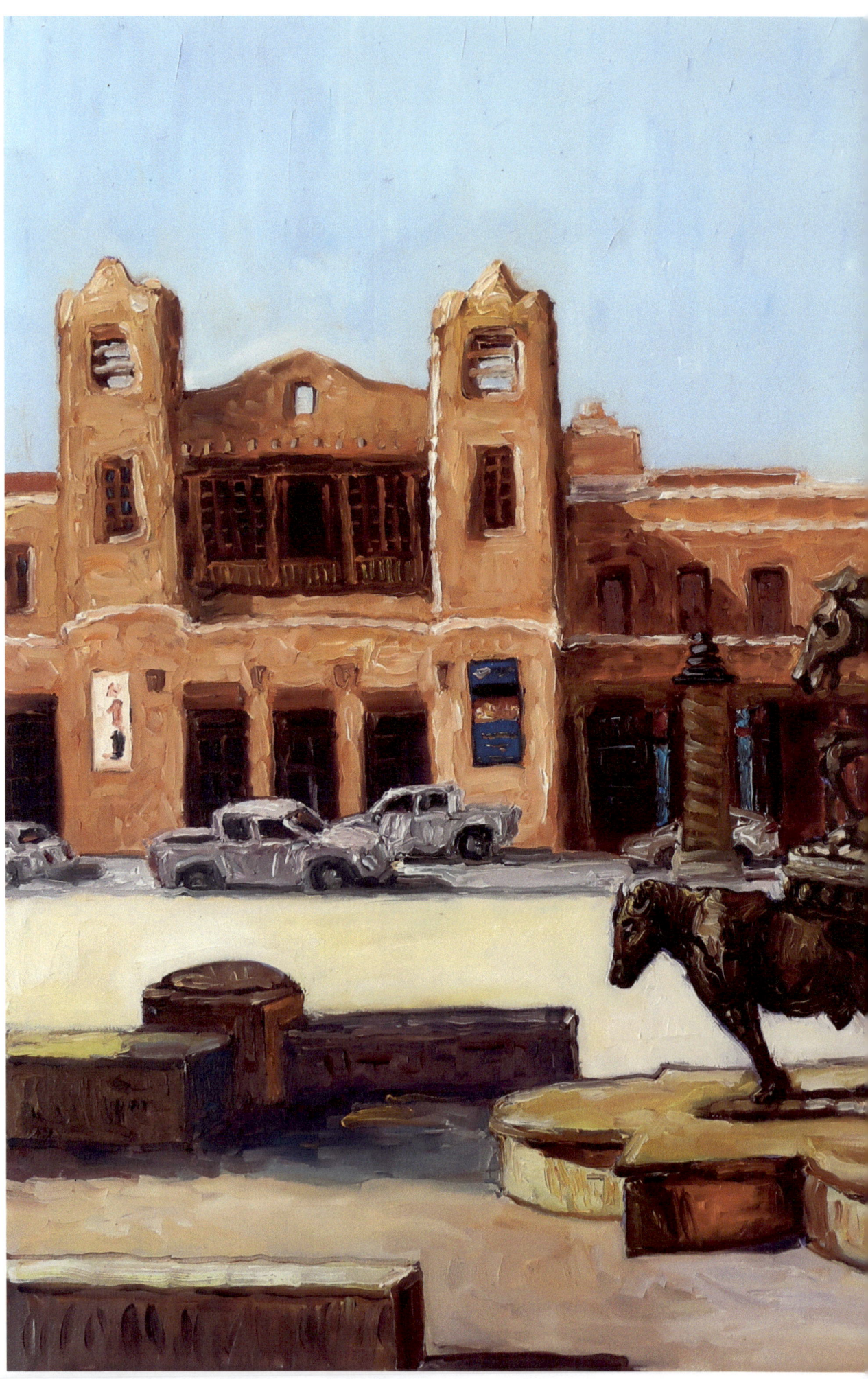

Ted Keller, a life-long artist, earned a BFA from Syracuse University in Ceramics and Painting, and then went on to receive an MFA from the University of Montana. In the five decades since receiving his degrees, Ted has taught art classes that were popular, even legendary, among his students in the several universities where he taught. He has made and sold over 100,000 pieces of colorful sculpture and pottery, working in both stoneware and porcelain. And, using oils as well as watercolors, Ted has created thousands of paintings.

In 2014, Ted published a book that distills the core of his teachings about painting and watercolor, as well as his ideas and philosophy concerning the process of becoming an artist. These ideas have a depth and simplicity that have inspired, and continue to inspire, students and beginning artists of all ages. The book is called <u>Watercolor: One Person's Teachings on Watercolor Painting and Becoming an Artist, Along With a Gallery of His Work</u> . The book is available directly from the author as well as on Amazon.

Over the past five years, Ted created a series of paintings about New York City, based on visits and photographs that he took there. However, more recently, Ted has settled artistically into his current residence in the Southwest. Attracted by the mountains, the sun, and the incredible light, Ted moved to Taos, New Mexico with his wife Peggy in 2008. Here is what he says about painting New Mexico:

"Having lived now for many years in Taos, the light, visual clarity, and the emptiness have become a part of me. I have learned to love the raggedy cottonwoods. The soft edges of the buildings in the southwest have come to be familiar. These things now appear in my paintings. I love to paint the ordinary and everyday scenes of the world. Using the painted surface, and the techniques of the application of the paint, I strive to bring life to the images I paint. If a painting is alive, it will always remain lively."

Ted lived in Maine for 35 years, selling his paintings and pottery at various galleries and shows throughout the course of that time. He is still represented by Carver Hill Gallery in Camden, Maine. The NYC paintings were featured in a two person successful show in the fall of 2021 at the Carver Hill Gallery. Ted feels that the foundation of his recent Southwestern paintings, strangely enough, was all that he experienced and learned in the creation of the New York City paintings.

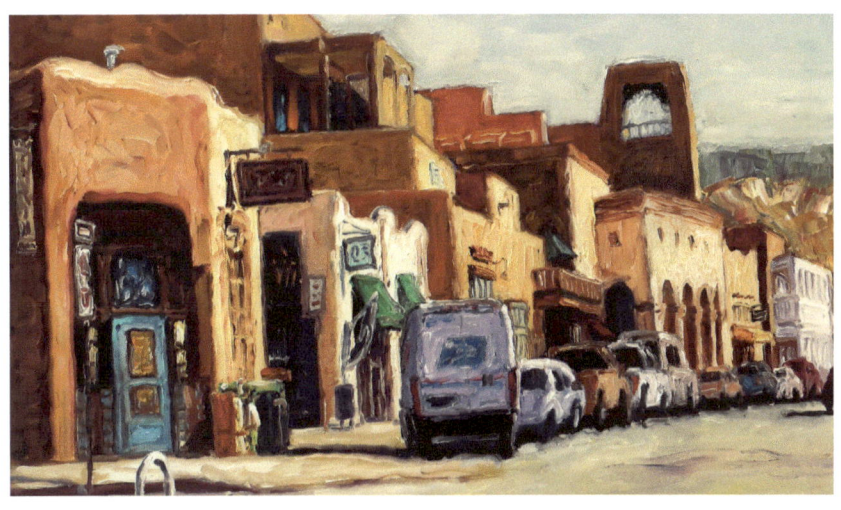

New Paintings Fall 2021 to Spring 2022

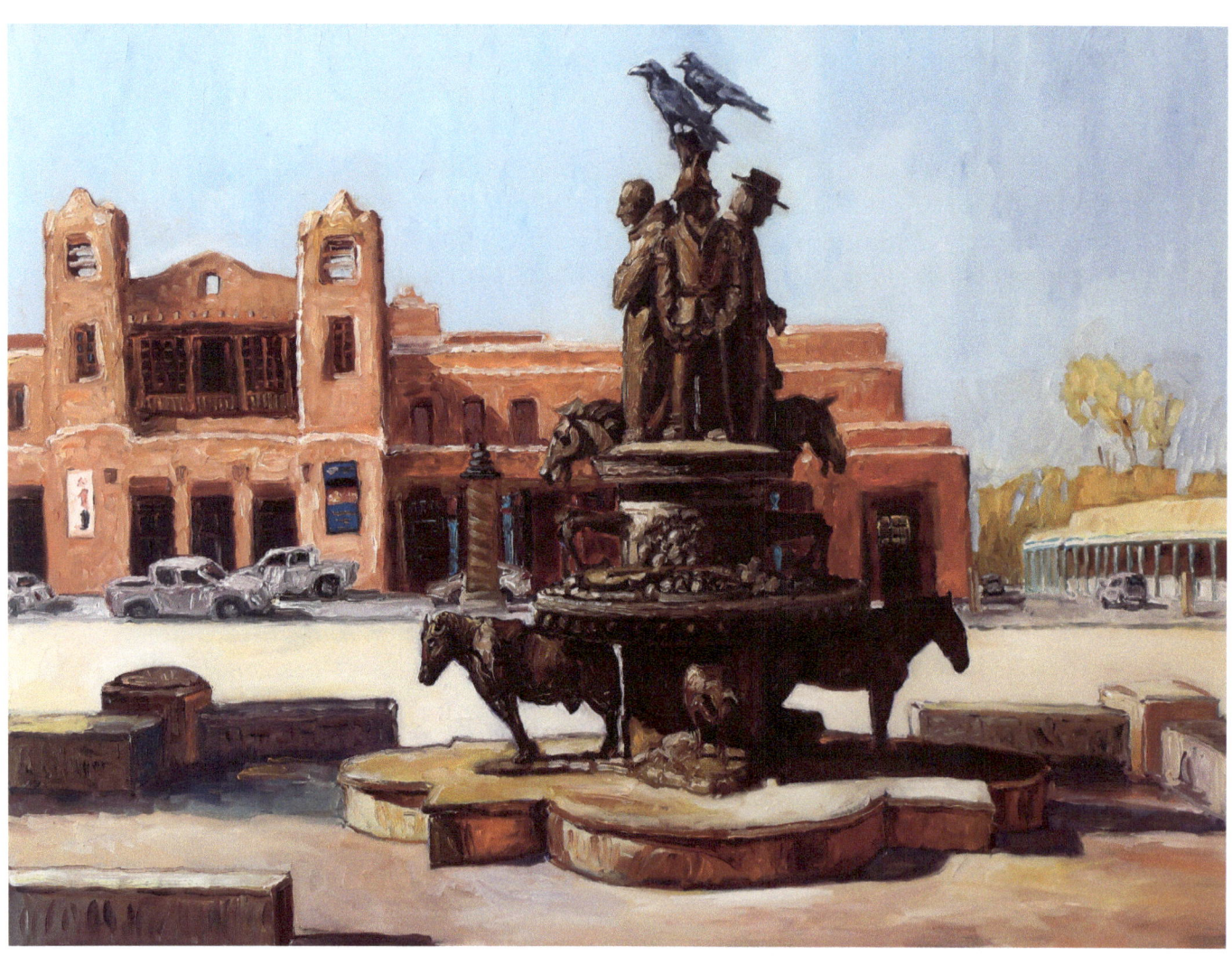

"Two Crows, Santa Fe" 43" x 31" oil on canvas

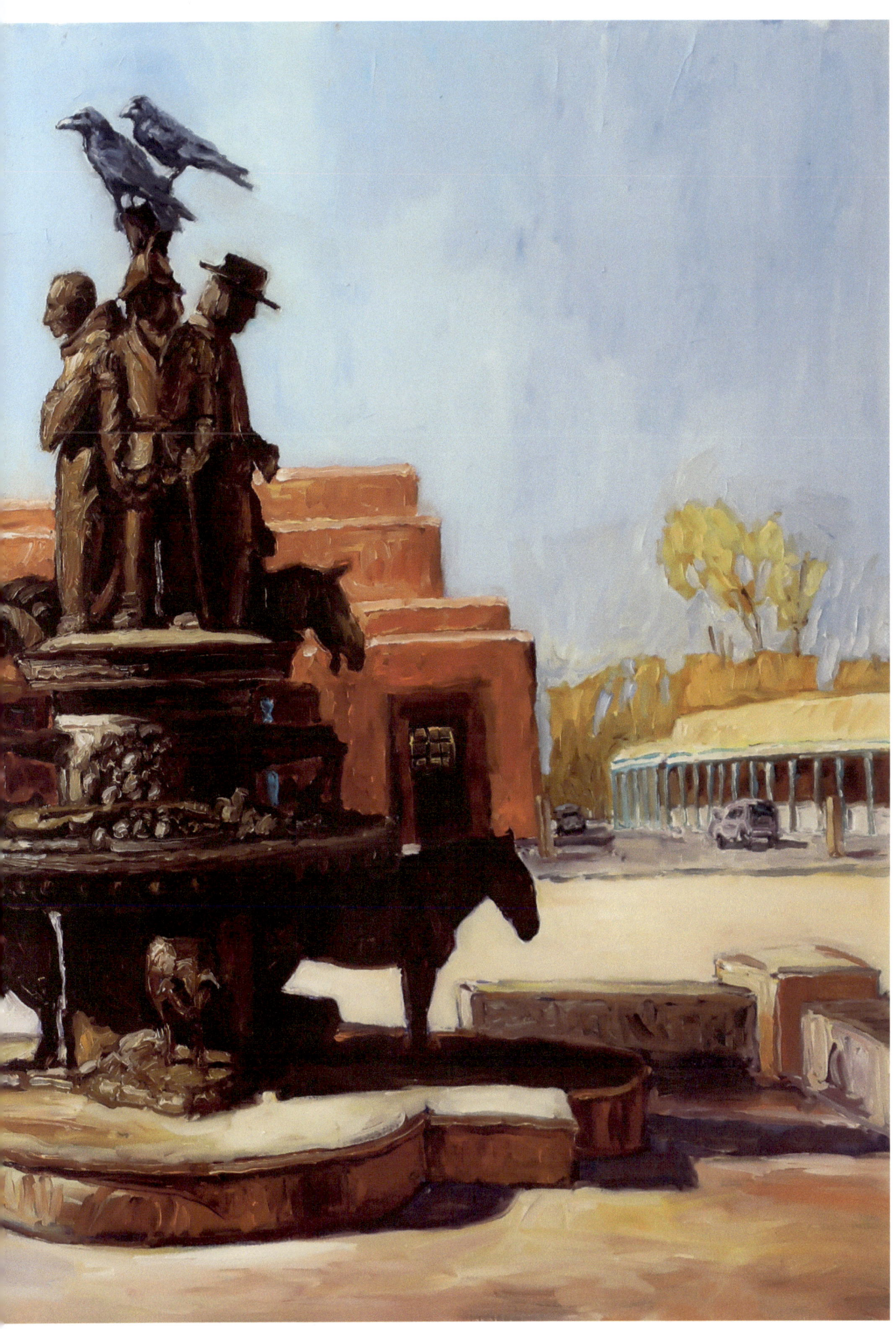

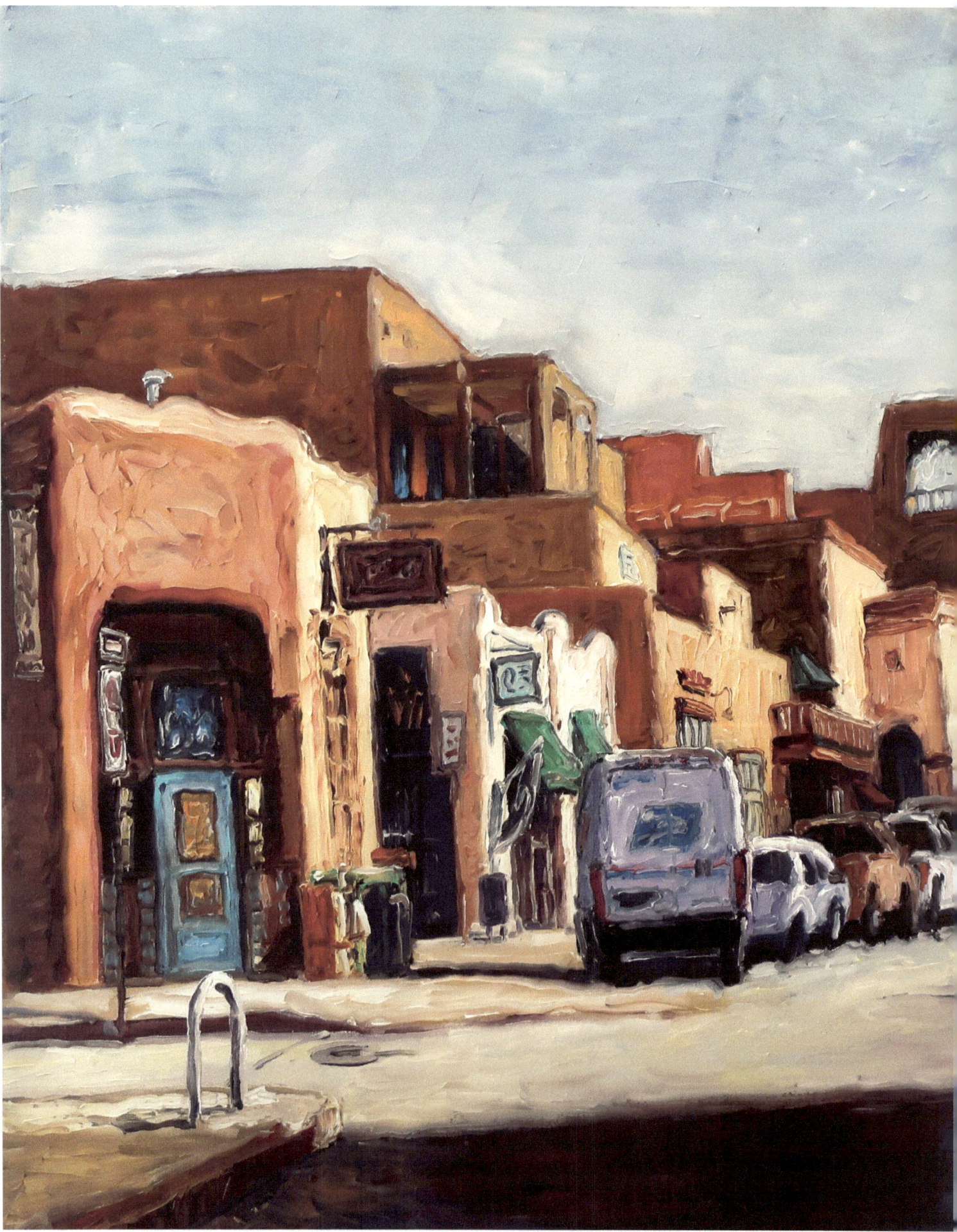

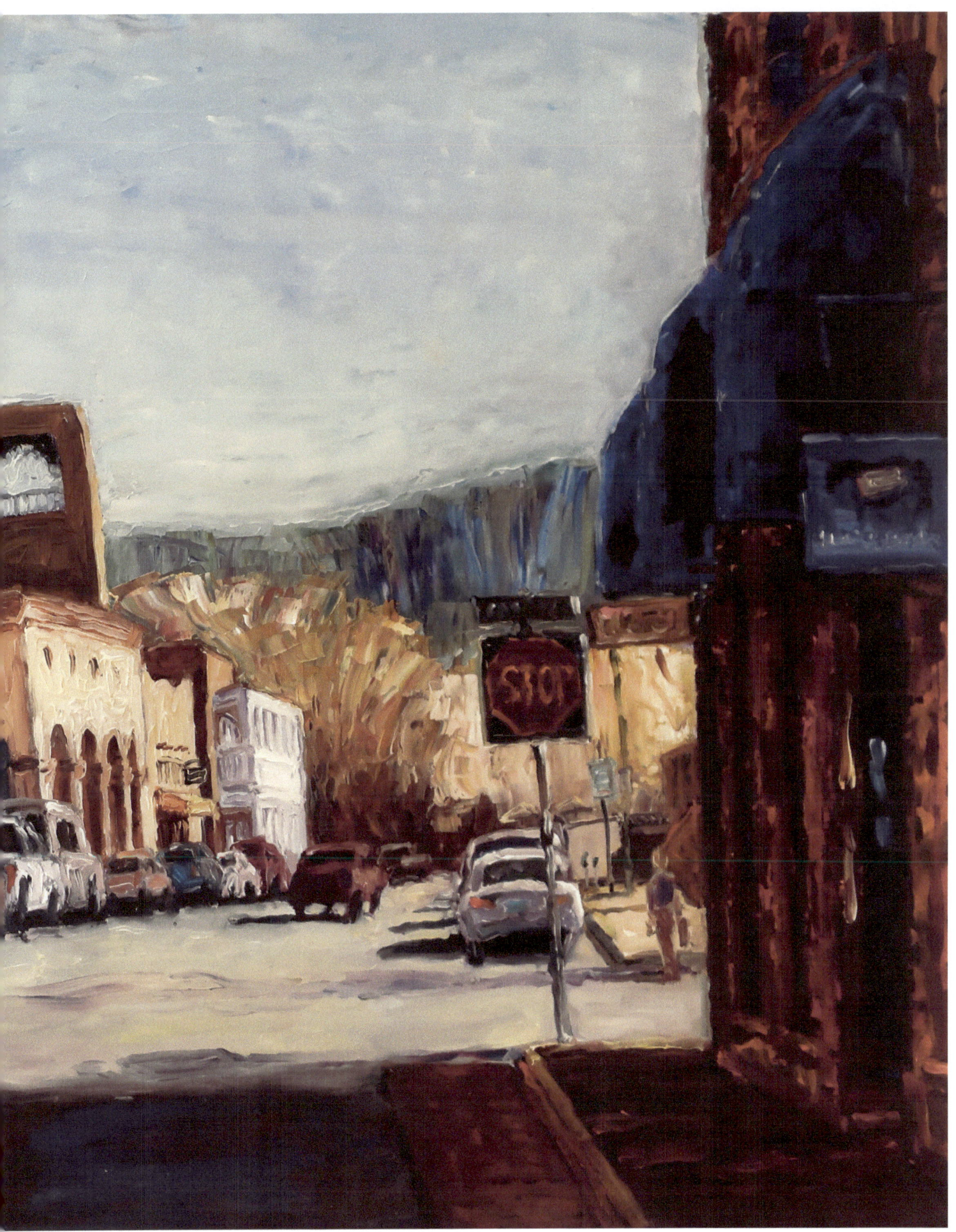

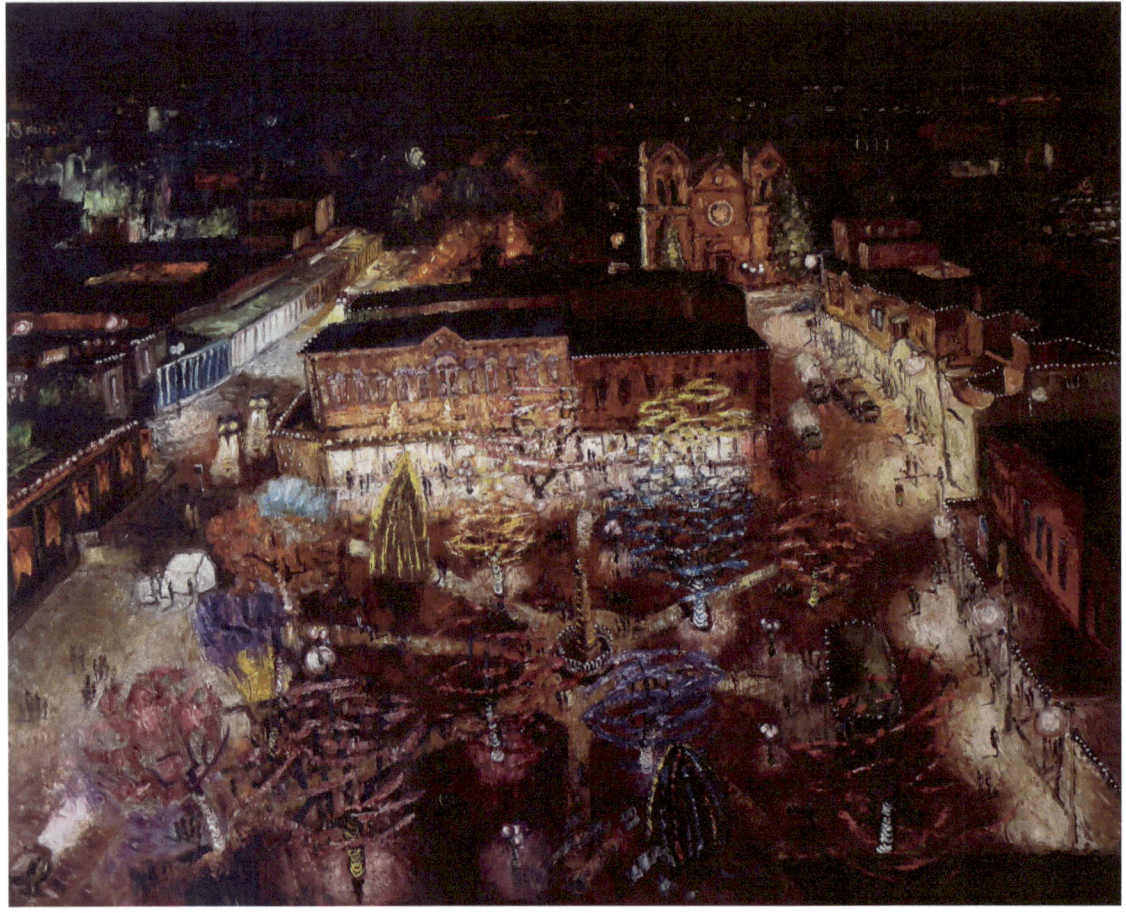

"Santa Fe Plaza, Holiday Lights"   54" x 42"   oil on canvas

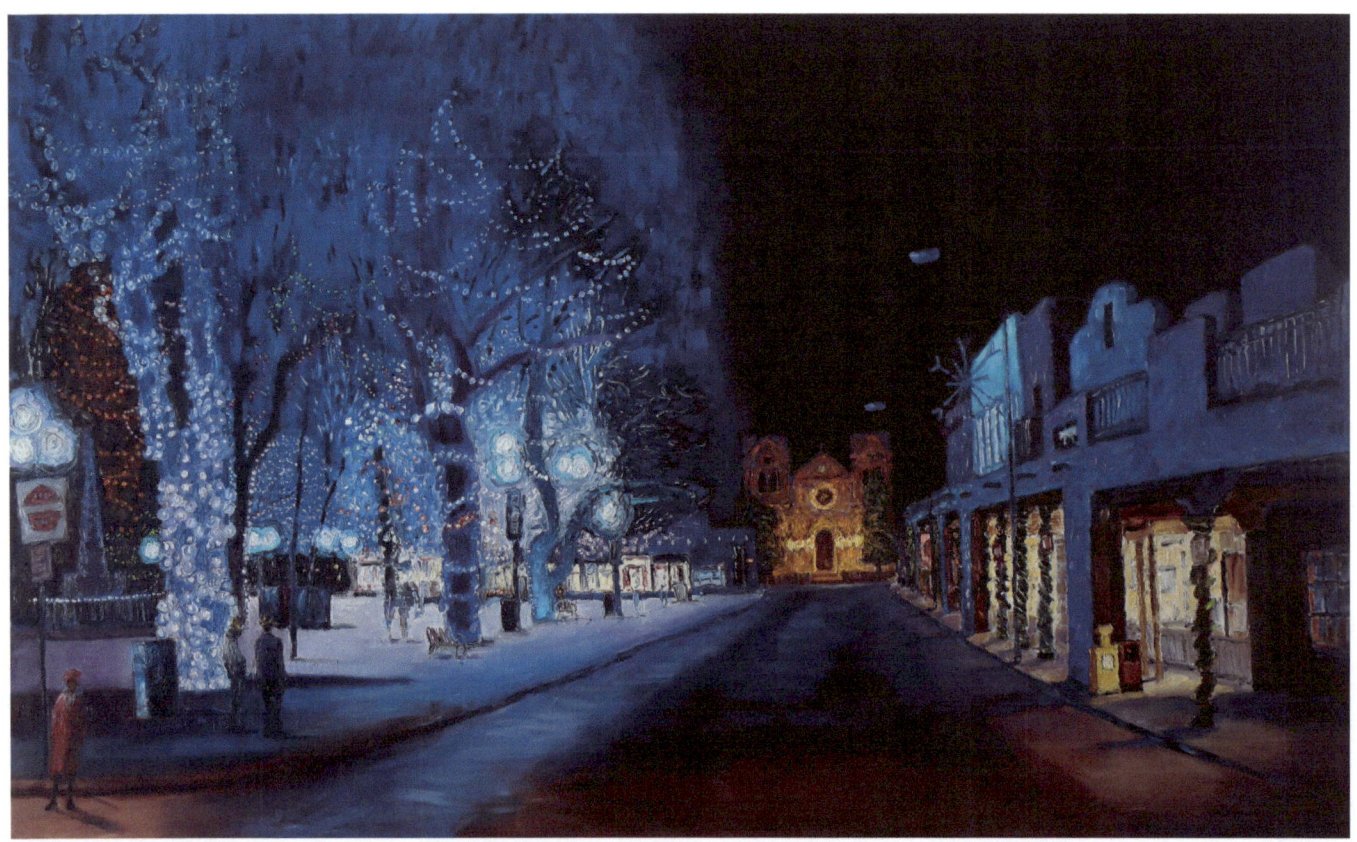

"Lady in Red, Santa Fe Plaza"   61" x 37"   oil on canvas

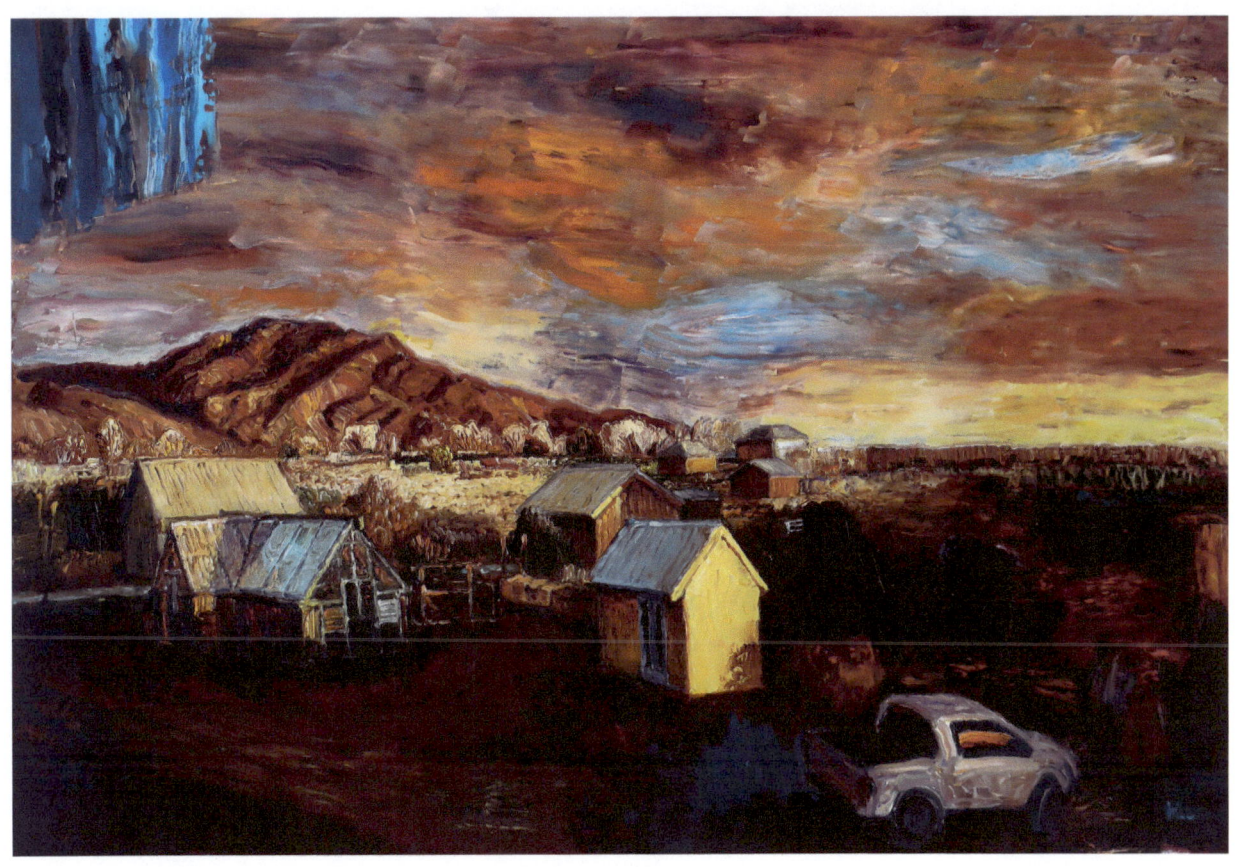

"View From the Deck, Taos"   54" x 36"   oil on canvas

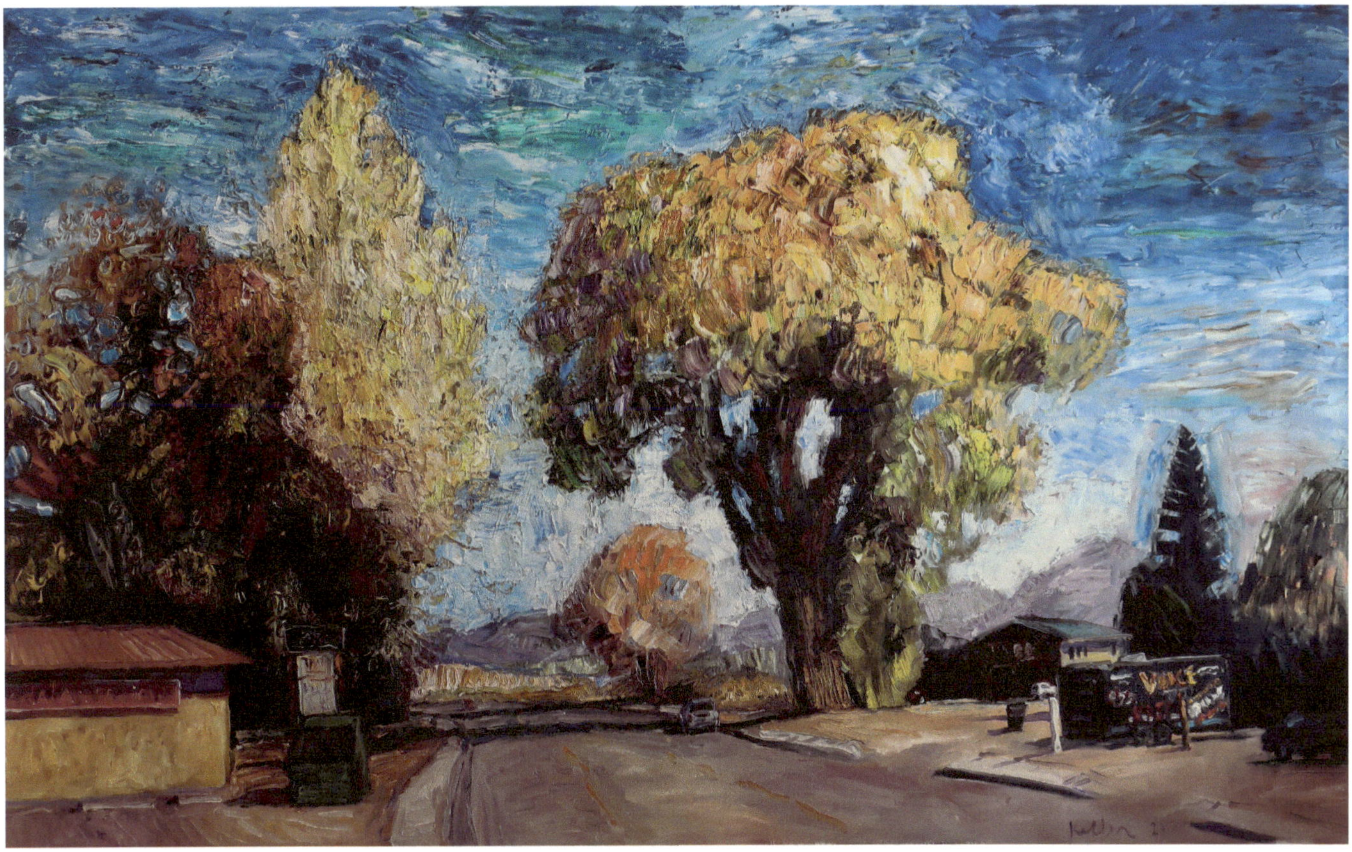

"Street Scene, Taos"   58" x 36"   oil on canvas

These 4 large paintings have expanded views on the following pages:

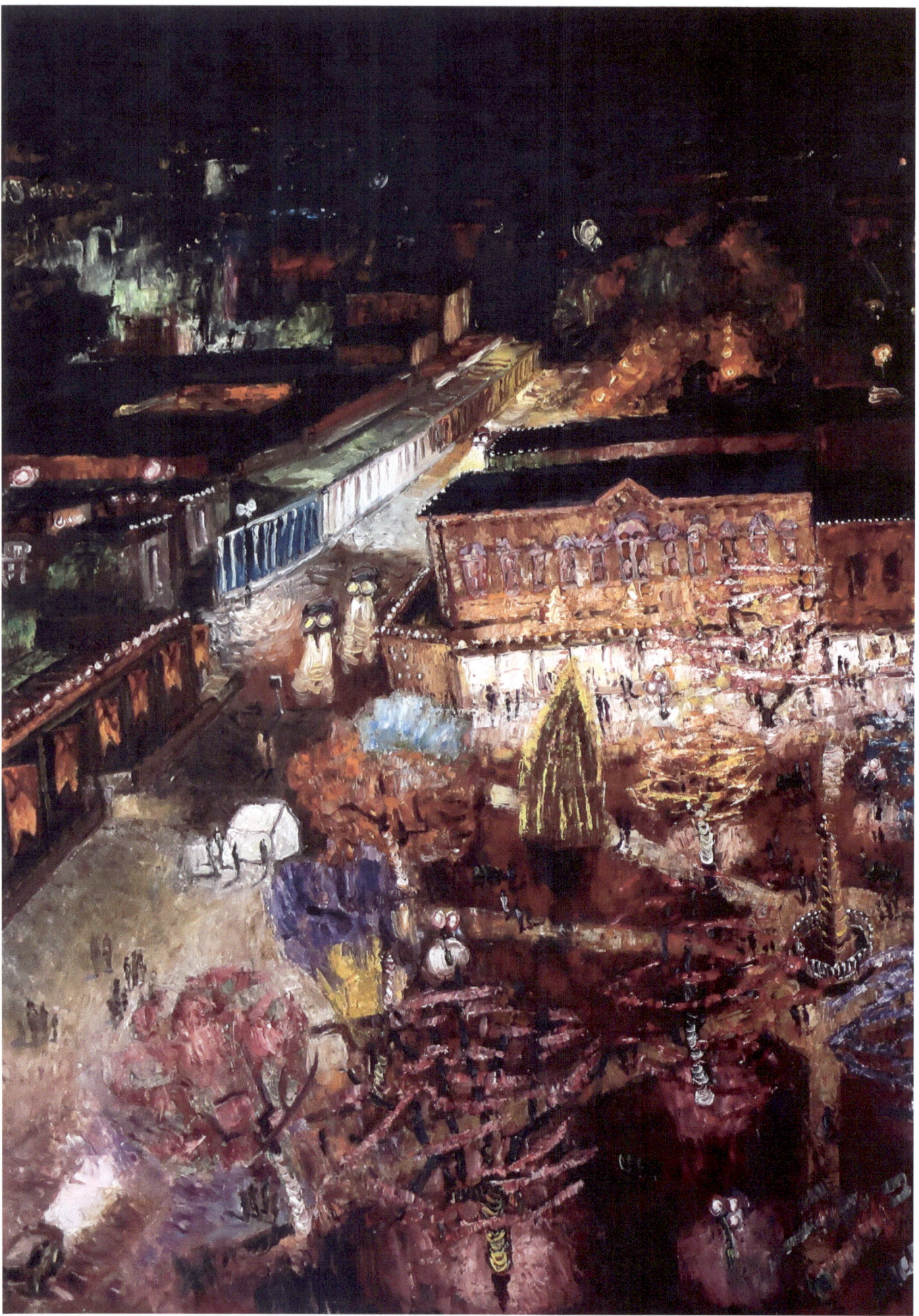

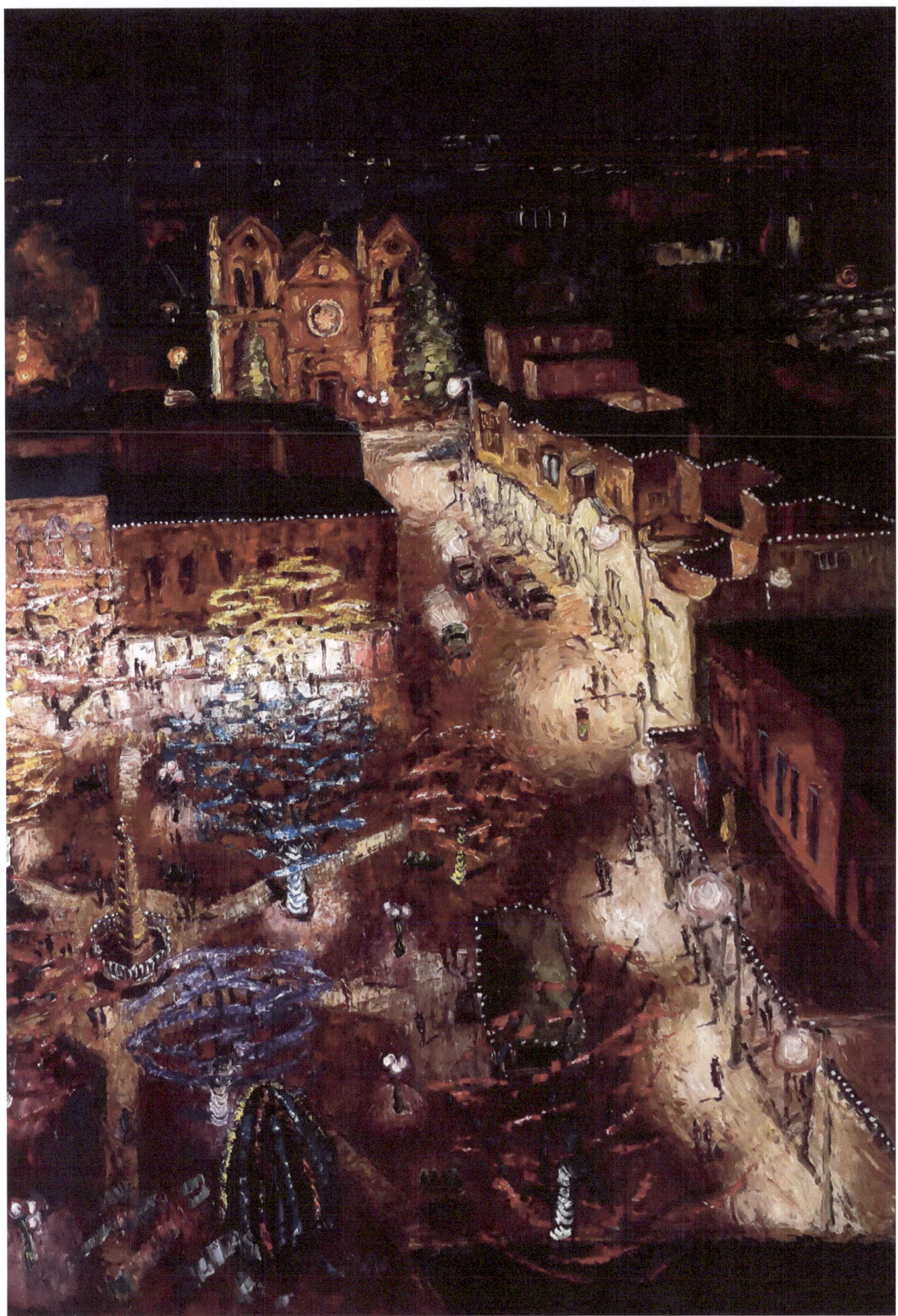

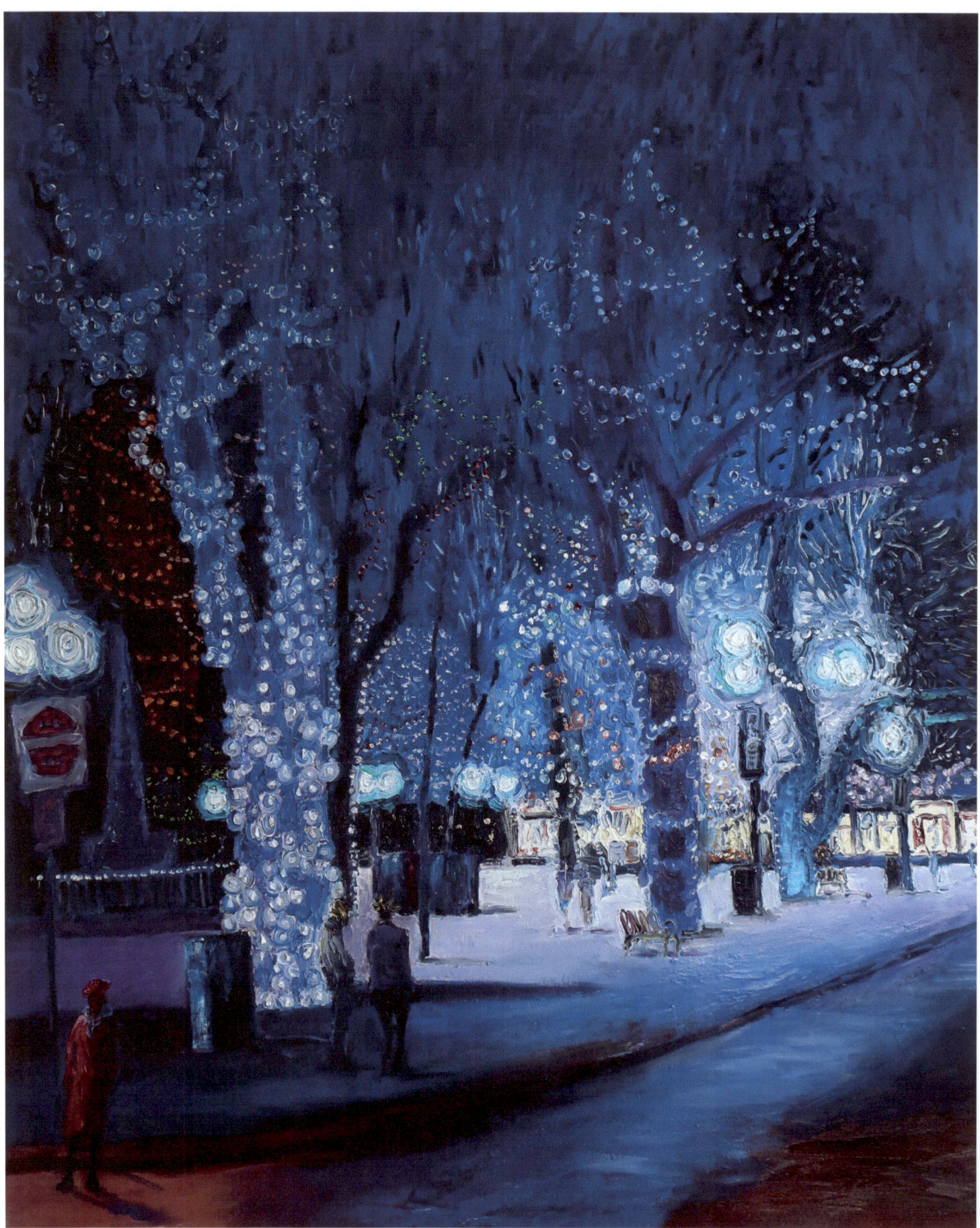

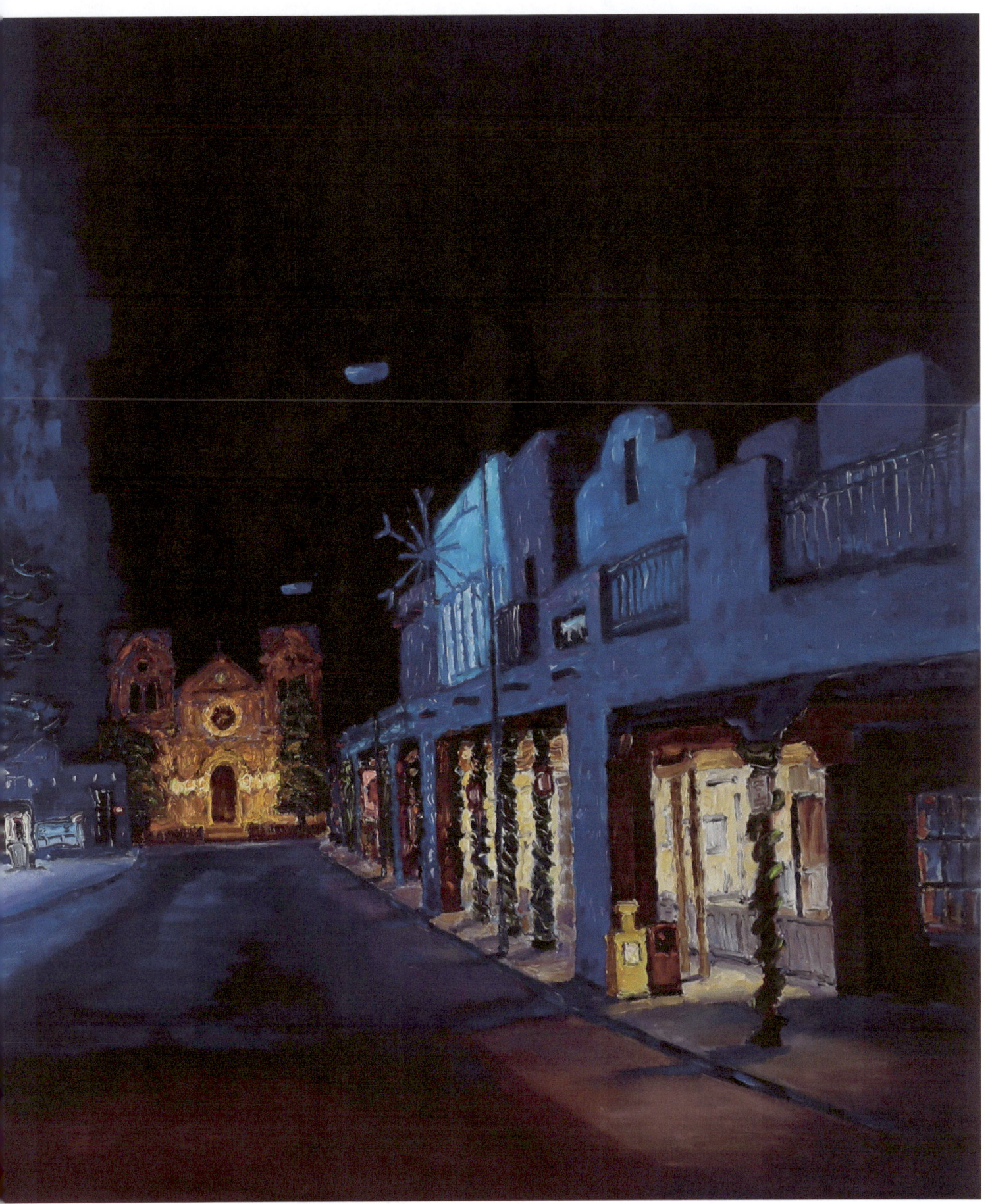

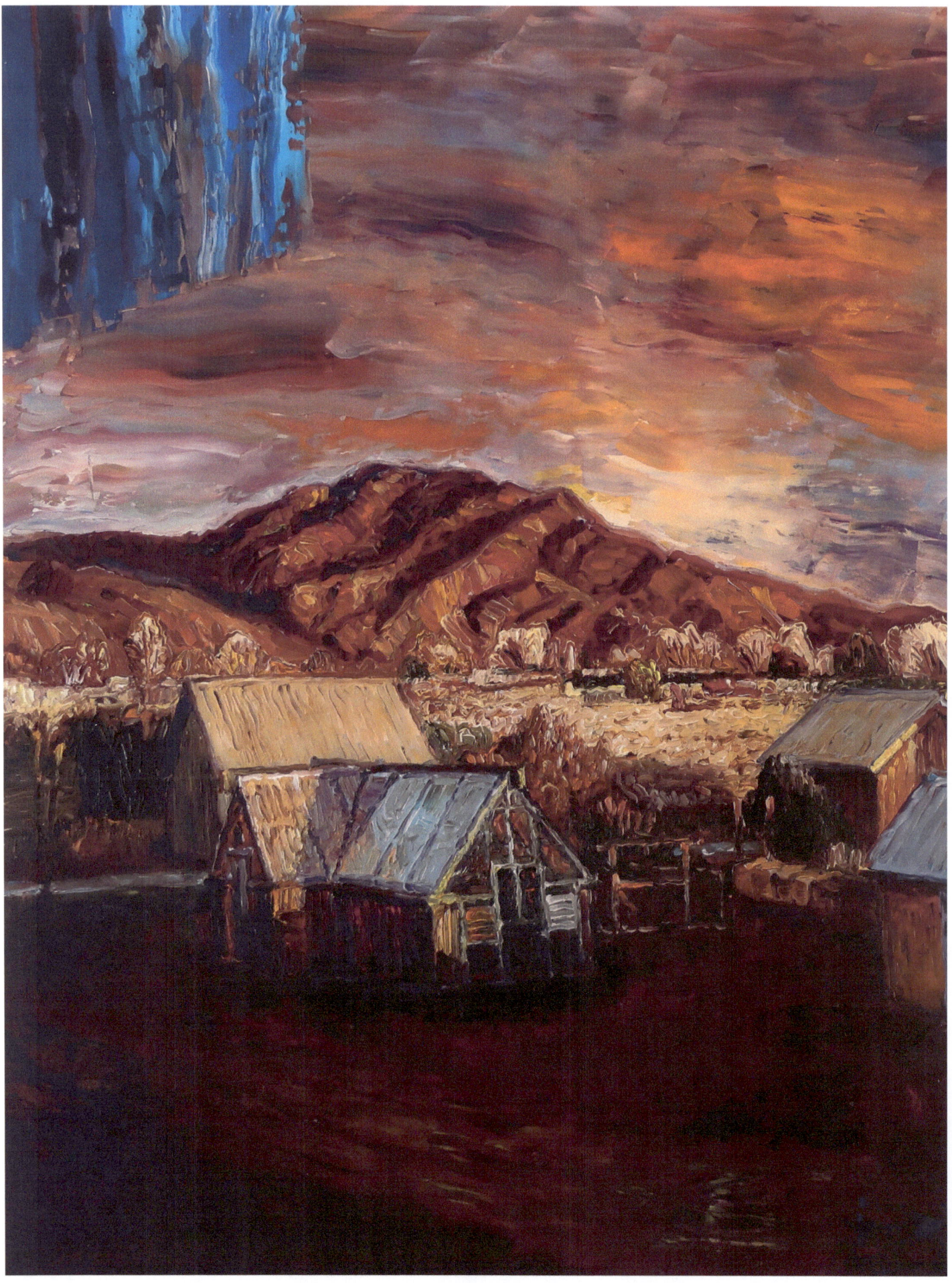

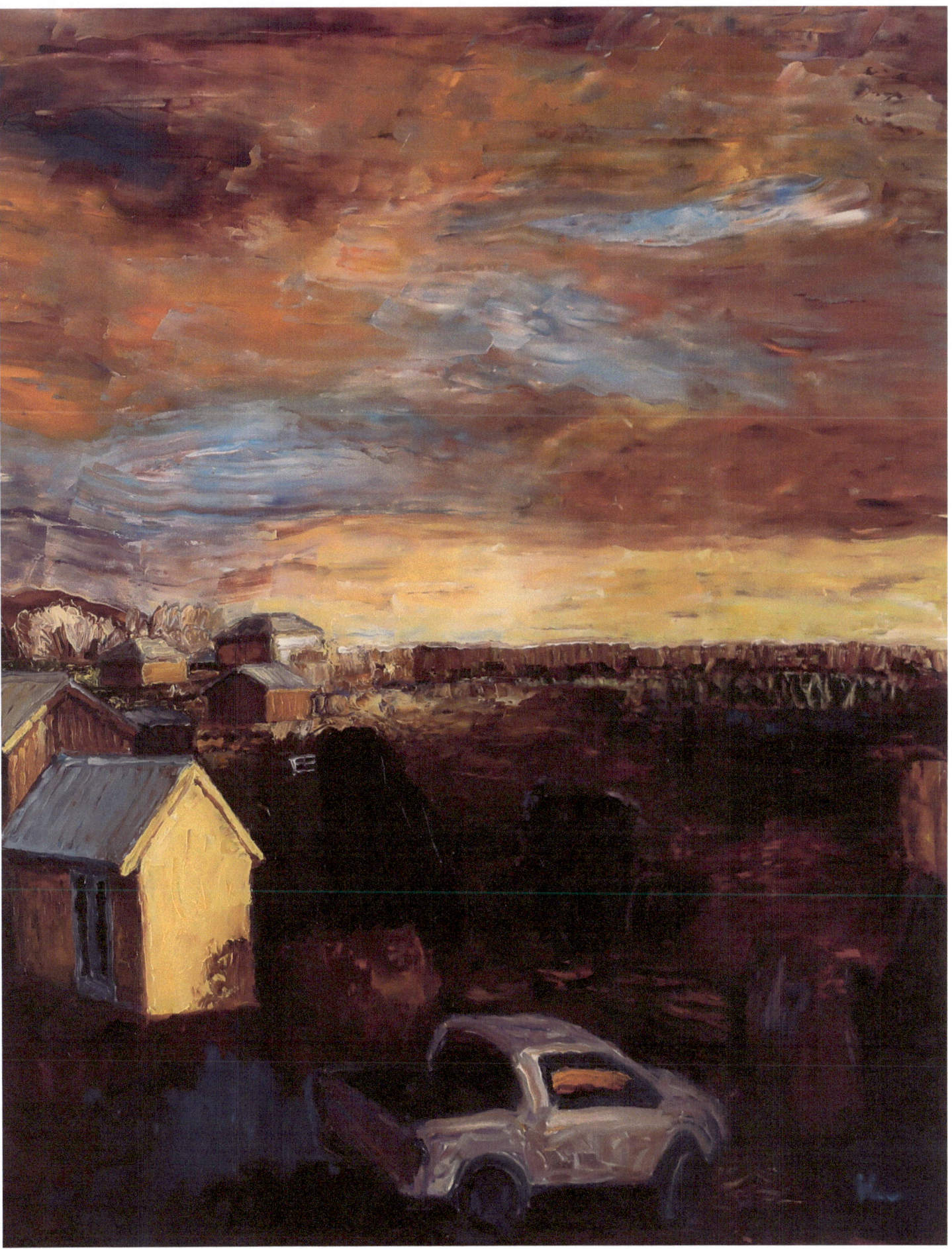

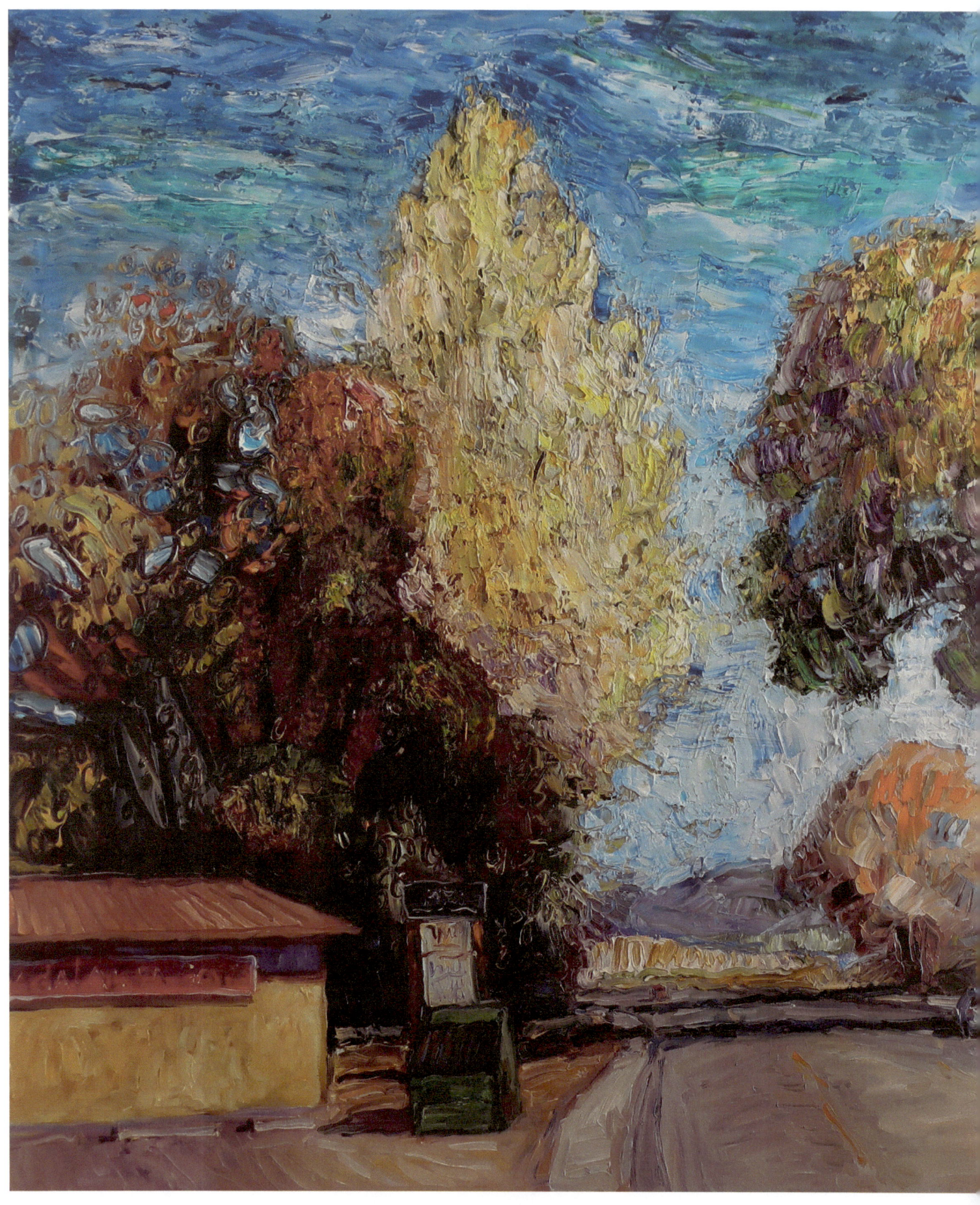

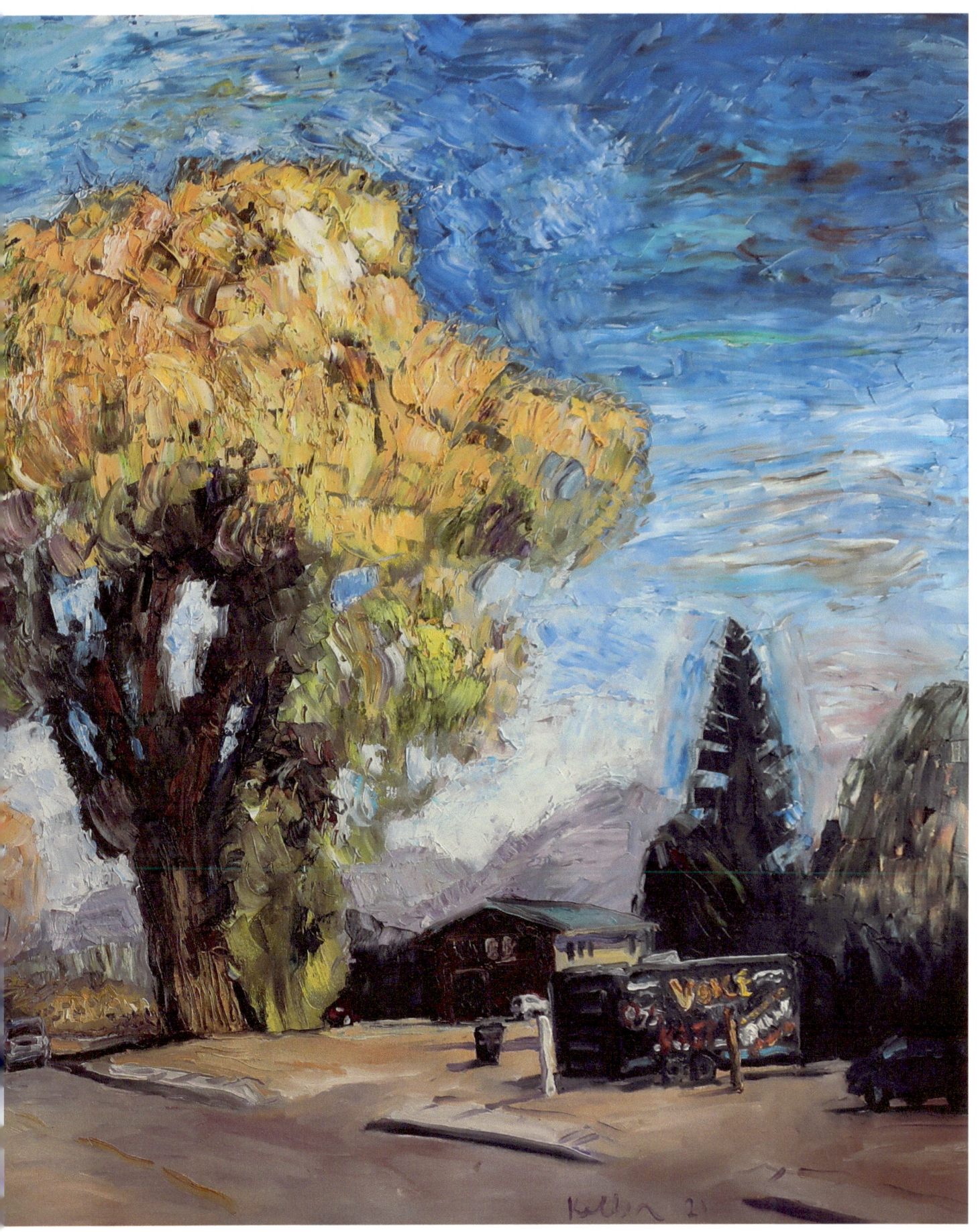

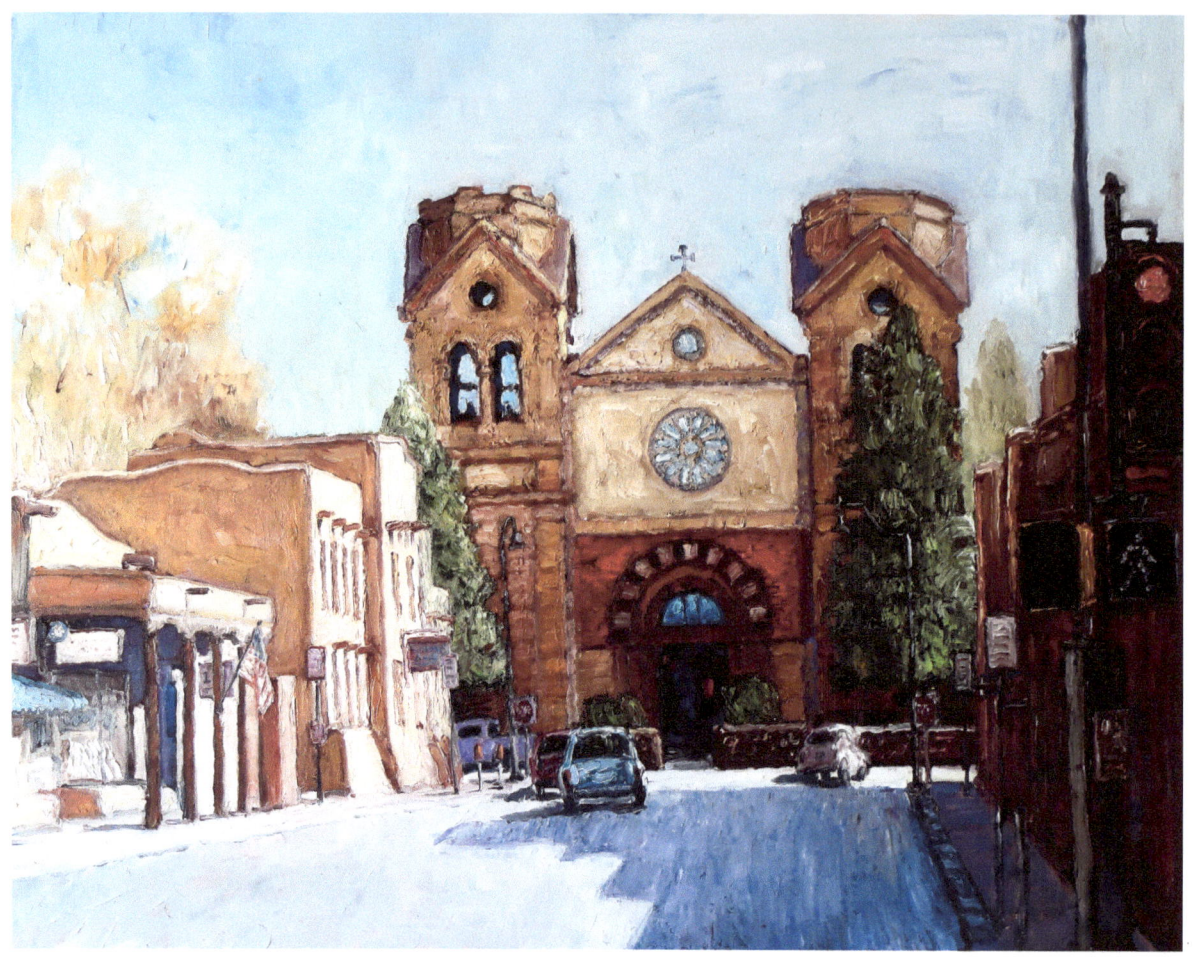

"Santa Fe Church" 38" x 30"   oil on canvas

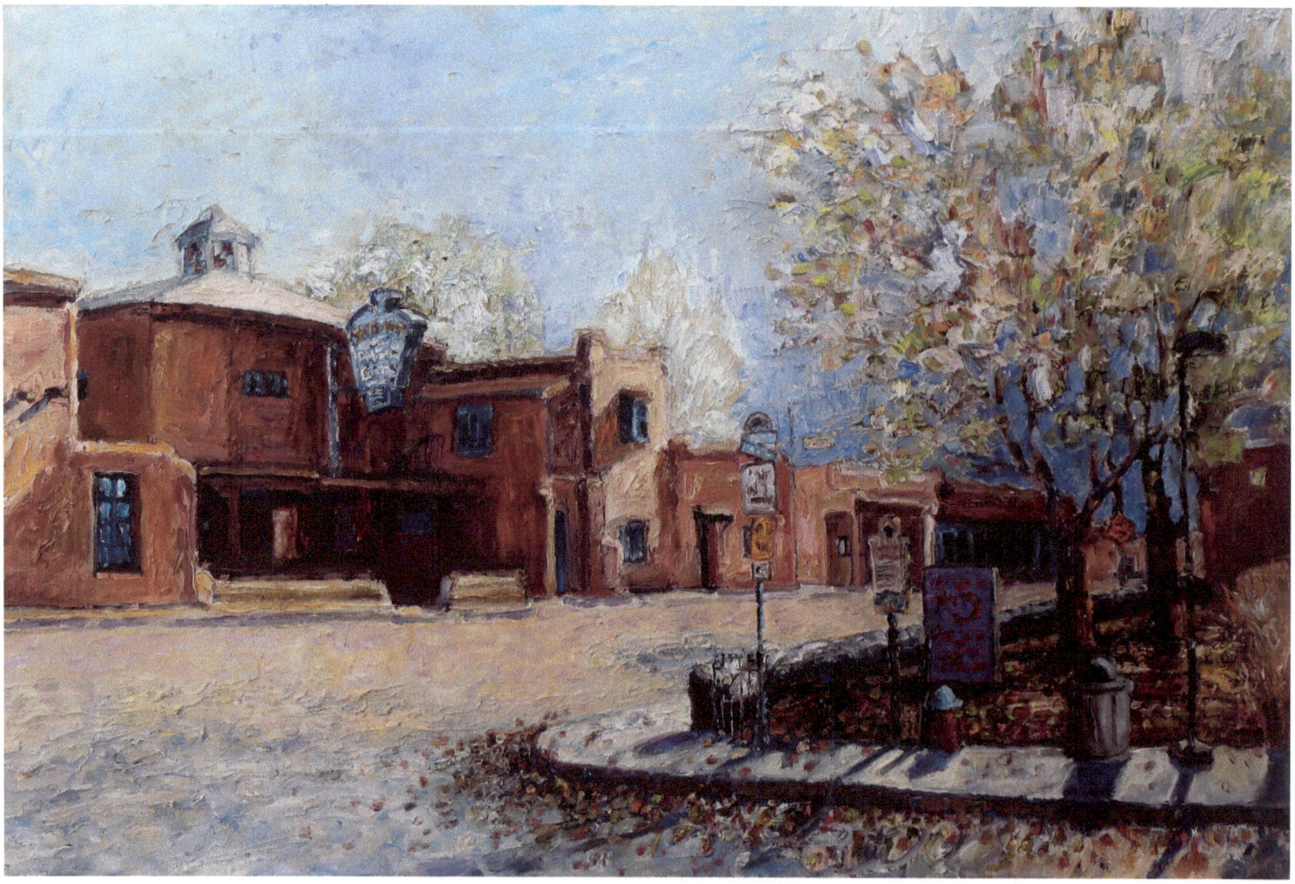

"Taos Inn" 38" x 25"   oil on canvas

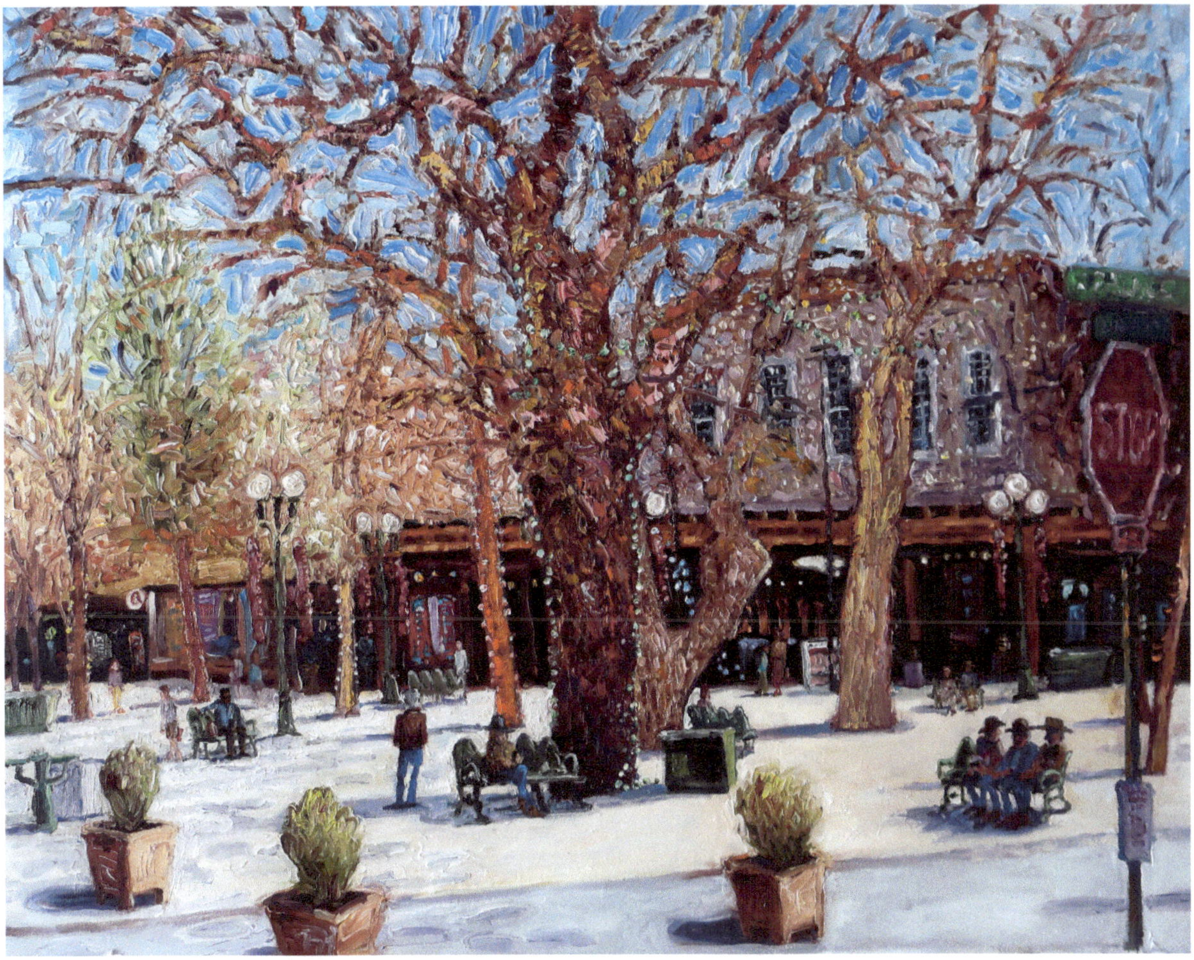

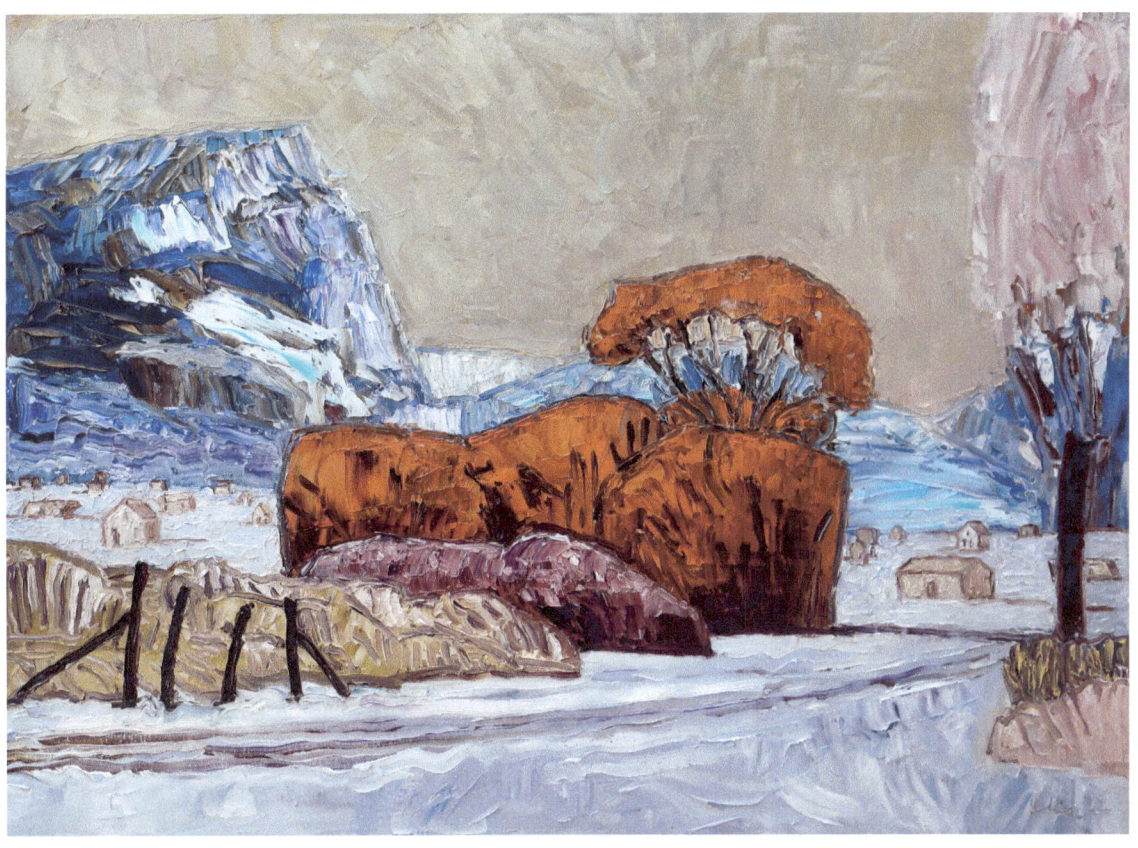

"Three Men on Santa Fe Plaza"   38" x 29"   oil on canvas

"Orange Trees, Arroyo Seco"   30" x 21"   oil on canvas

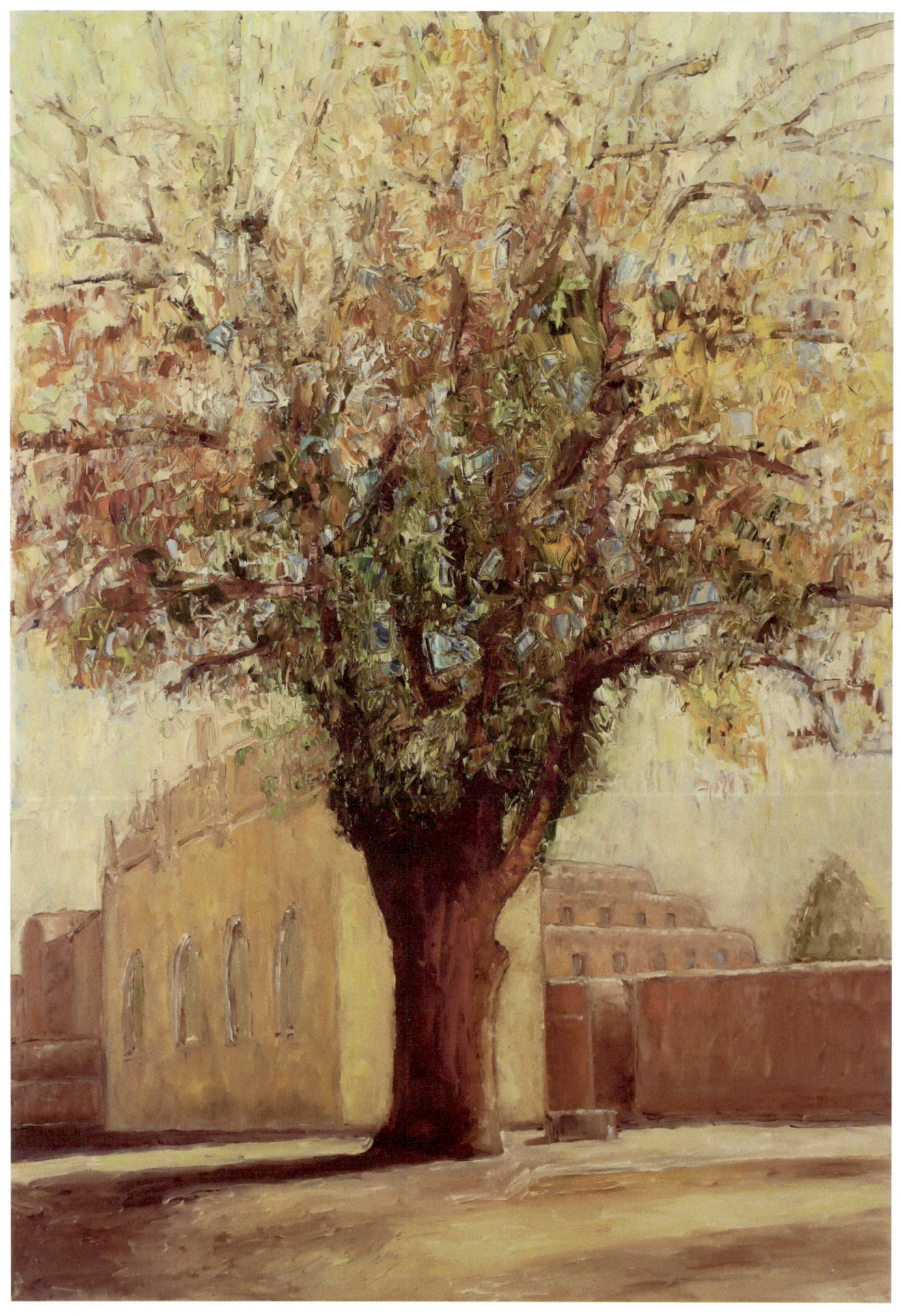

"Old Cottonwood in Santa Fe"　41" x 31"　oil on canvas

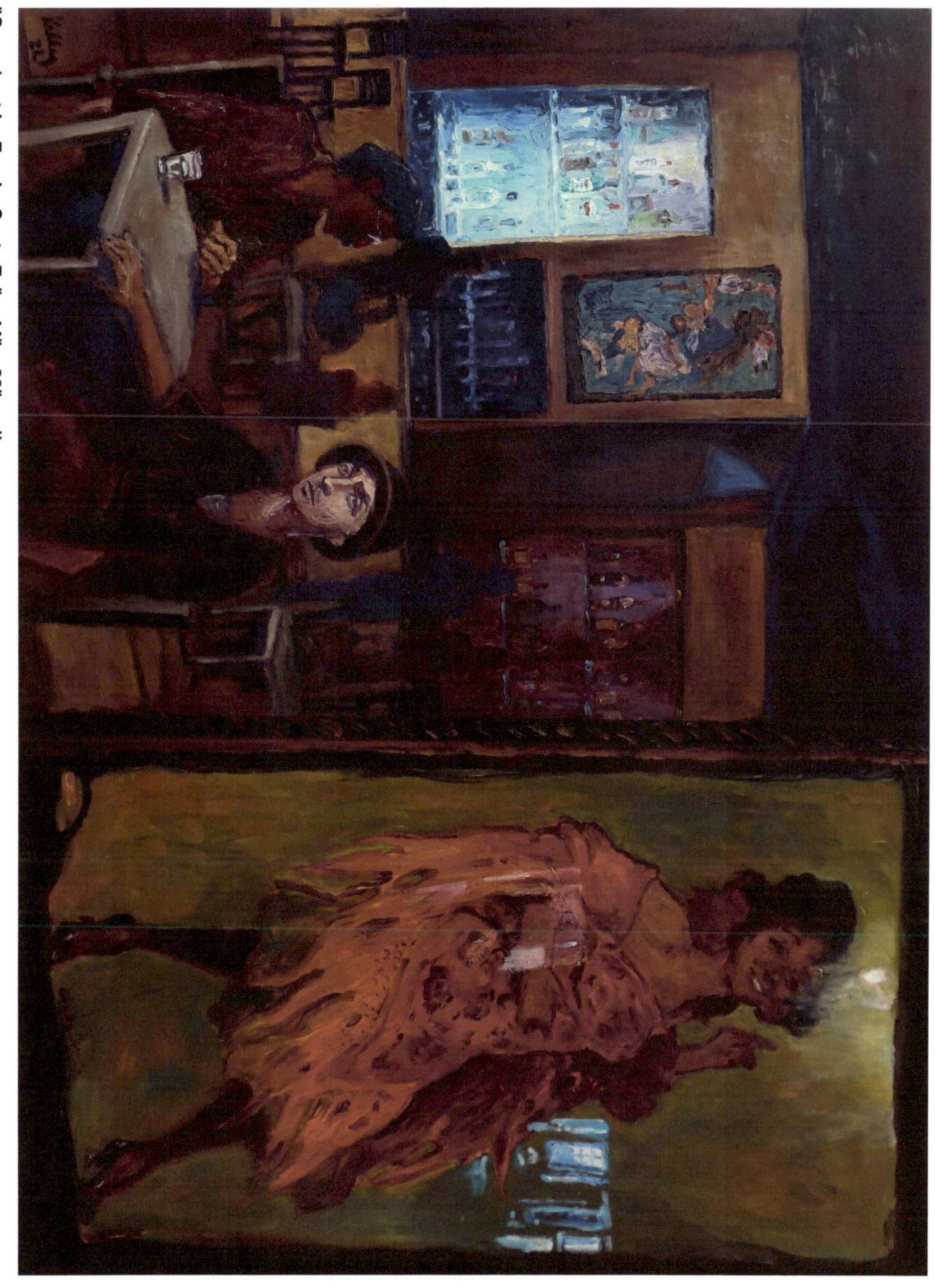

"Georgia at La Fonda, Santa Fe" 44" x 33" oil on canvas

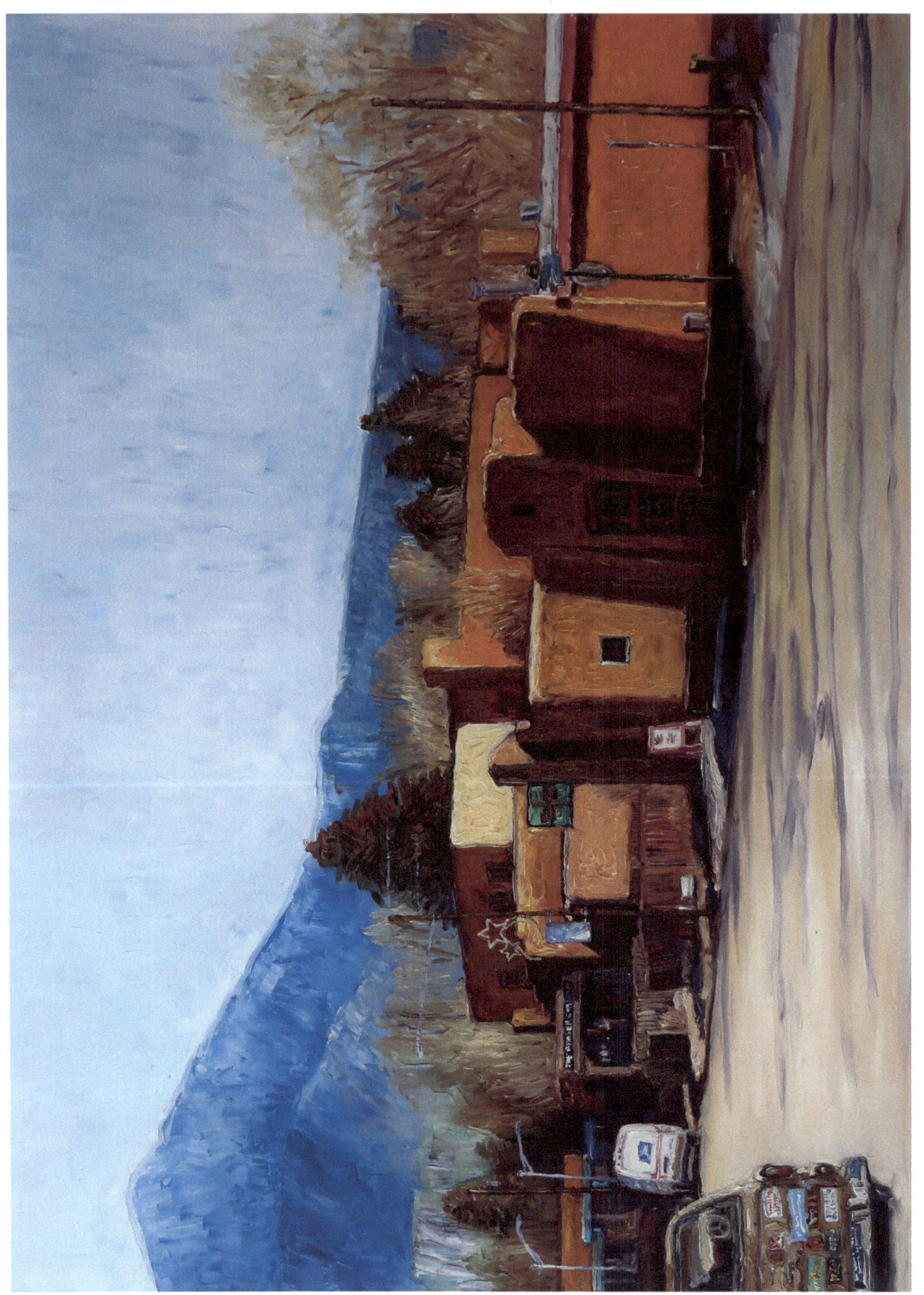

"Taos Street with Mail Truck" 43" x 32" oil on canvas

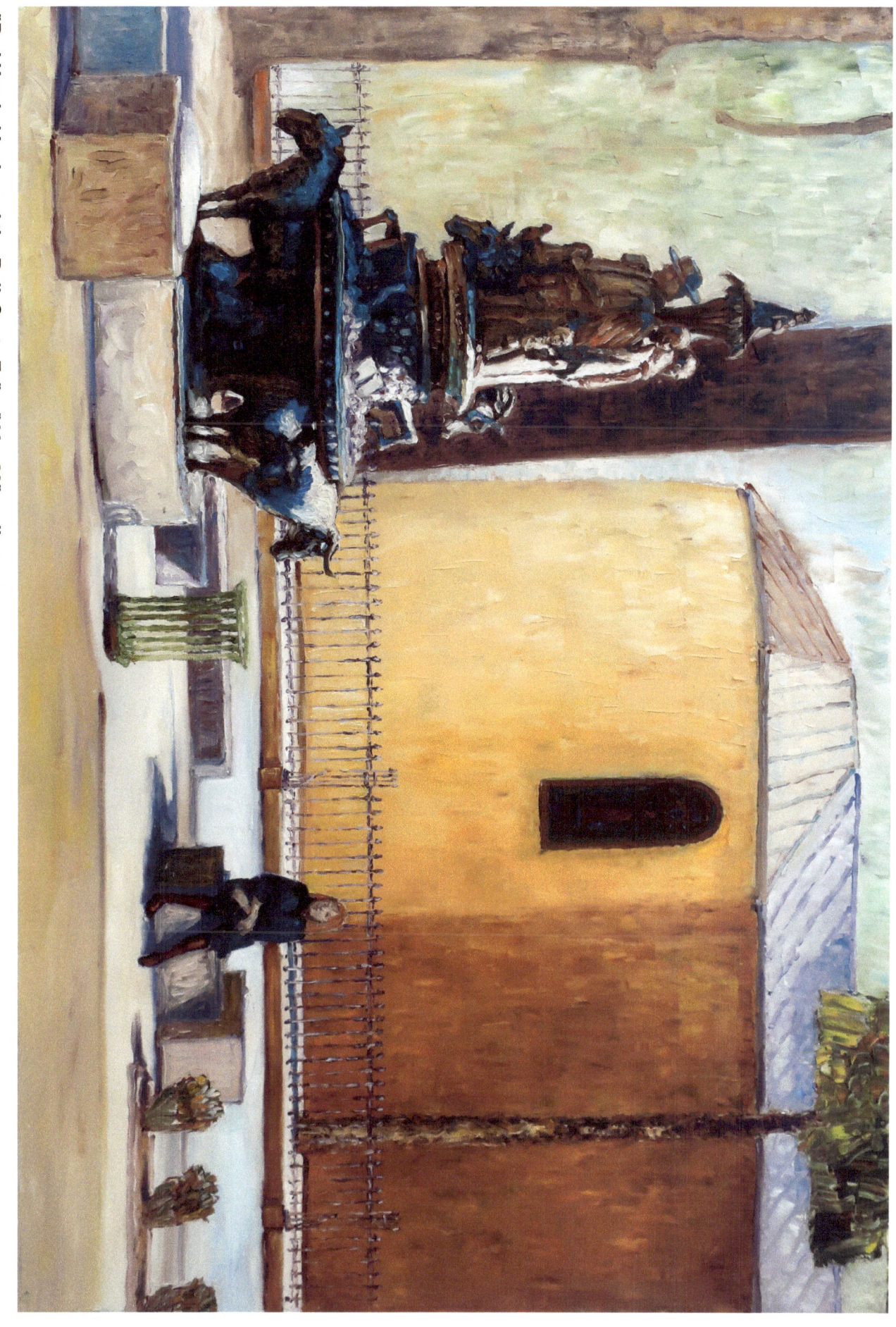

"Red Headed Lady and the Bull, Santa Fe" "44 x 30" oil on canvas

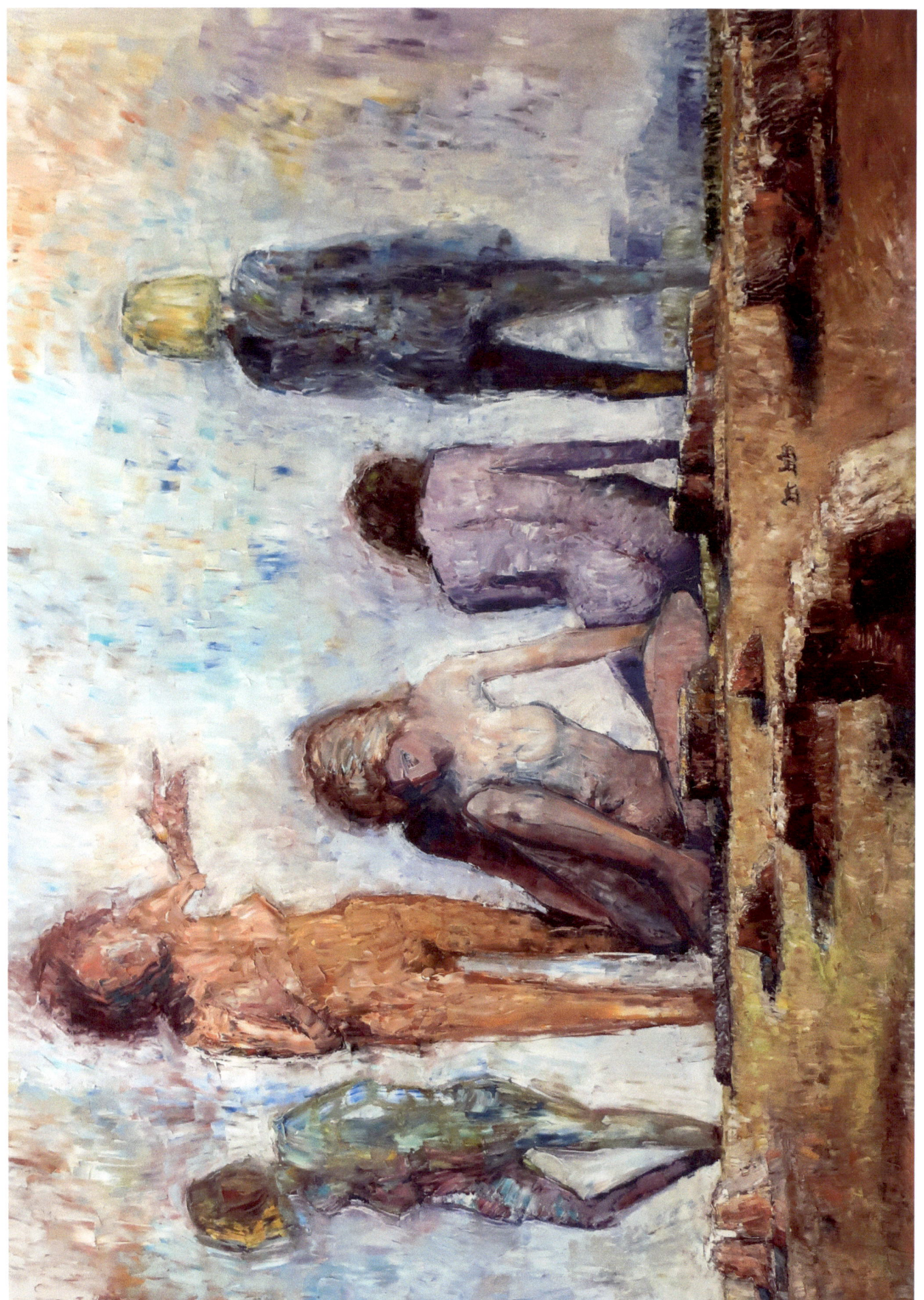

"Lady Giants and Three Horses"   61" x 43"   oil on canvas

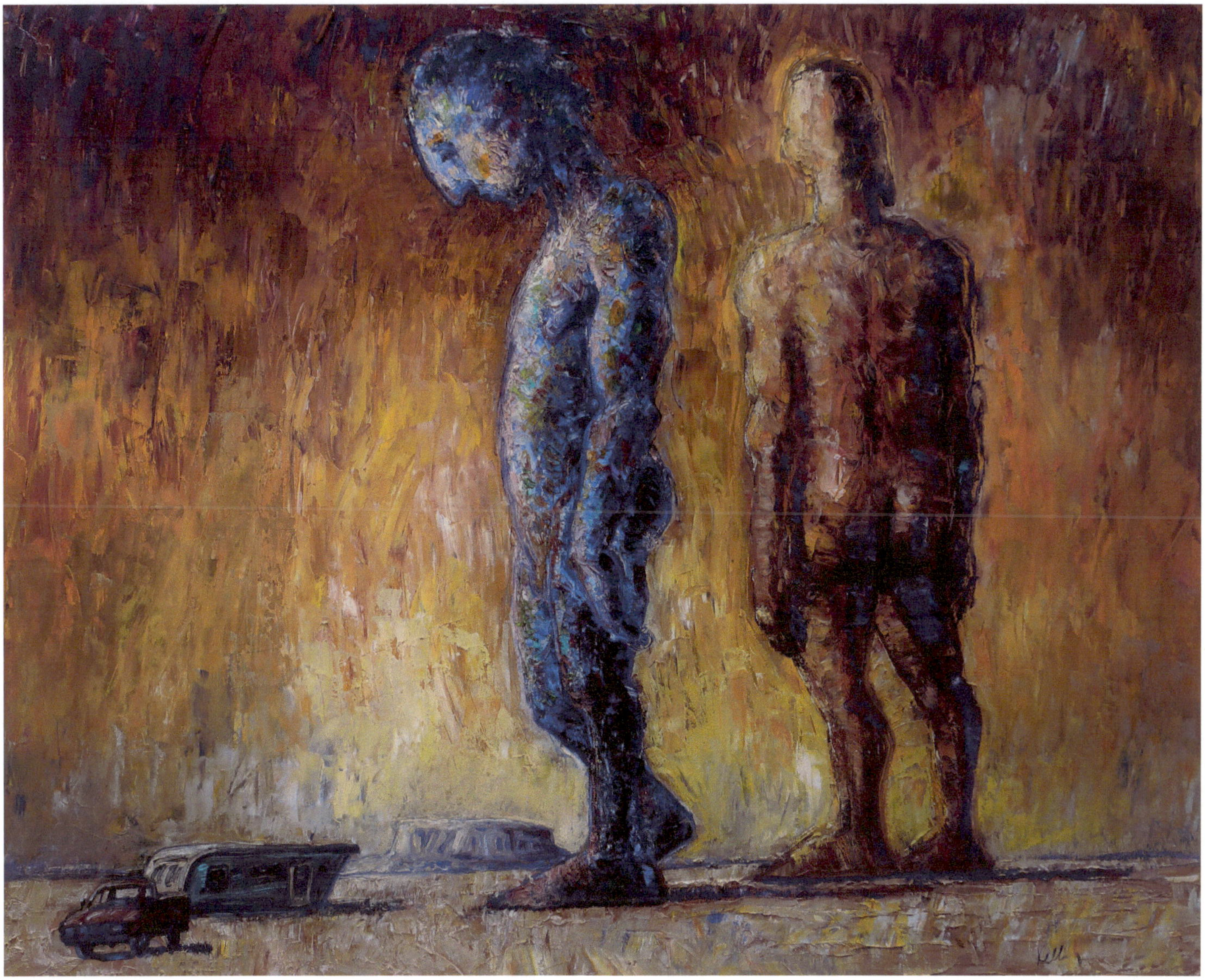

"Giants and the Trailer"   30" x 24"   oil on Arches

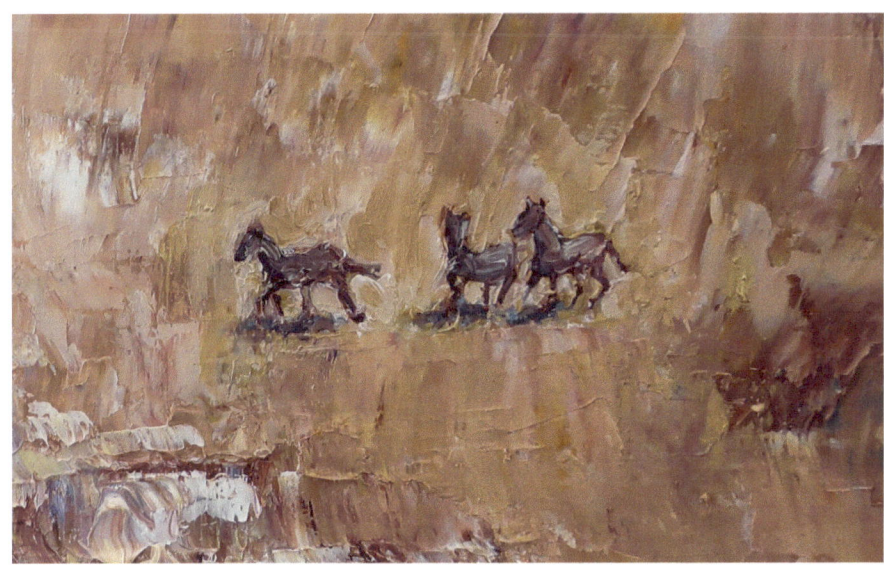

Lady Giants detail,   Three Horses

Earlier Oils, New Mexico

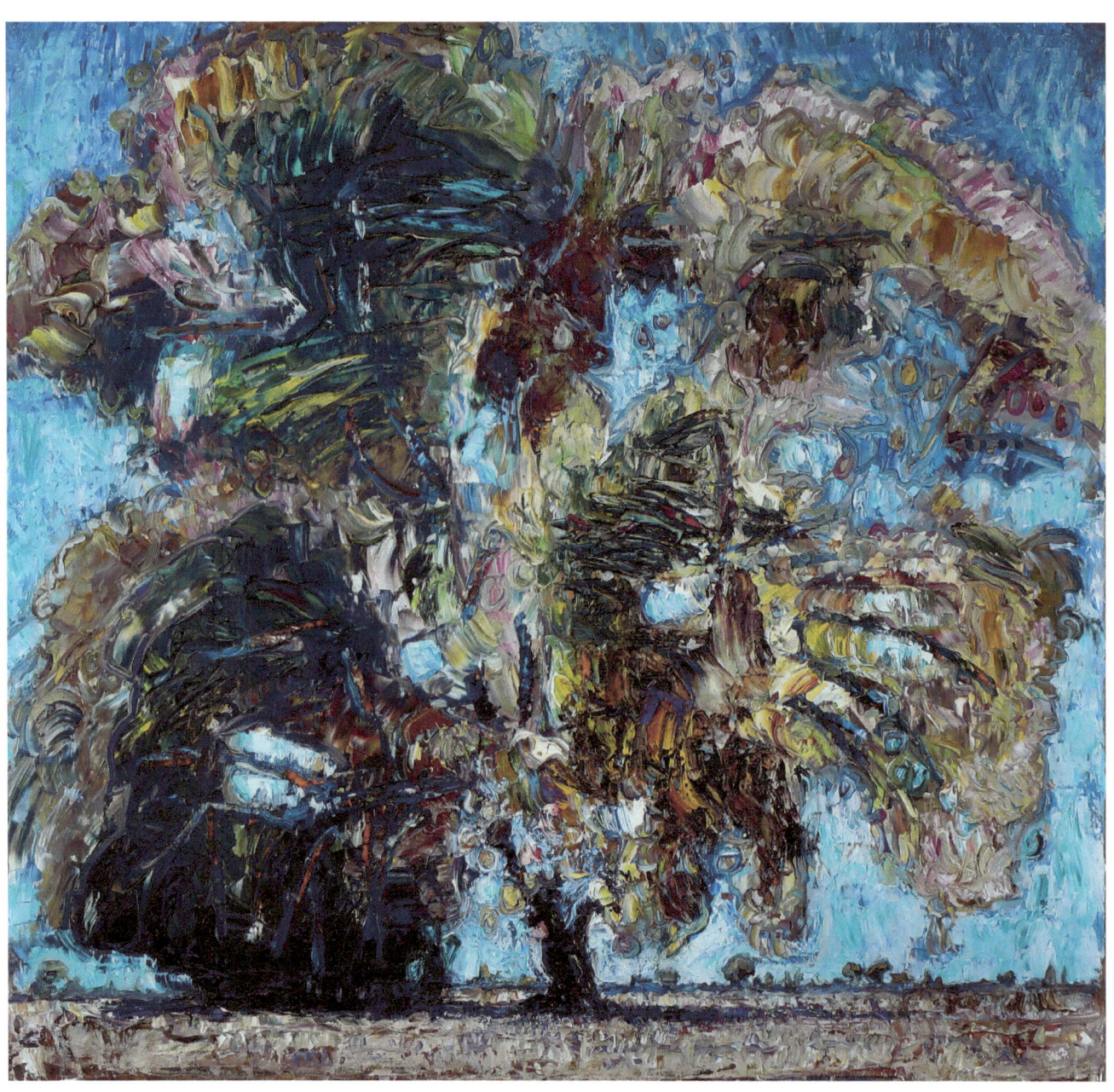

"Cottonwood, Turquoise Sky"   22" x 21"   oil on Arches

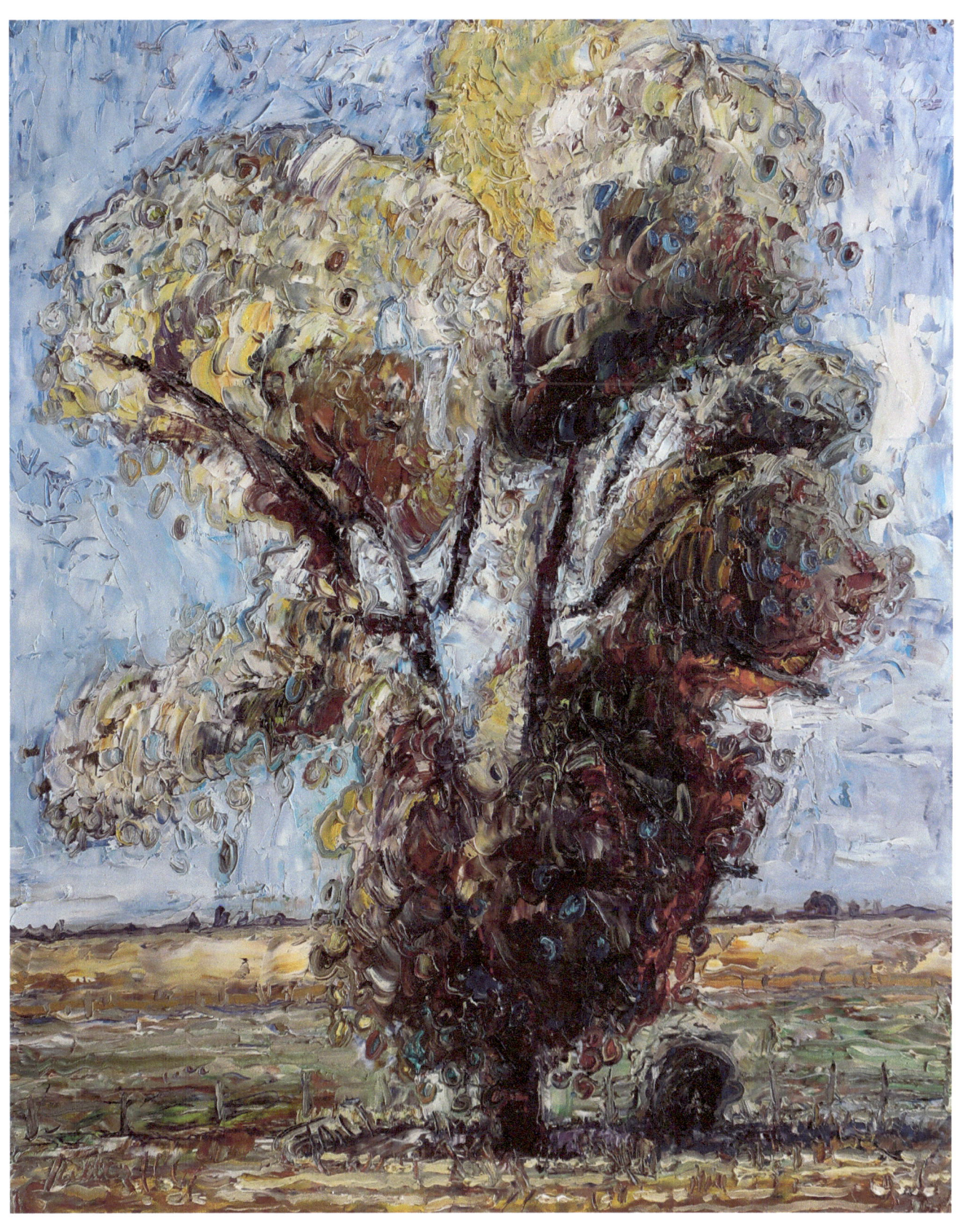

"Cottonwood"   22" x 18"   oil on Arches

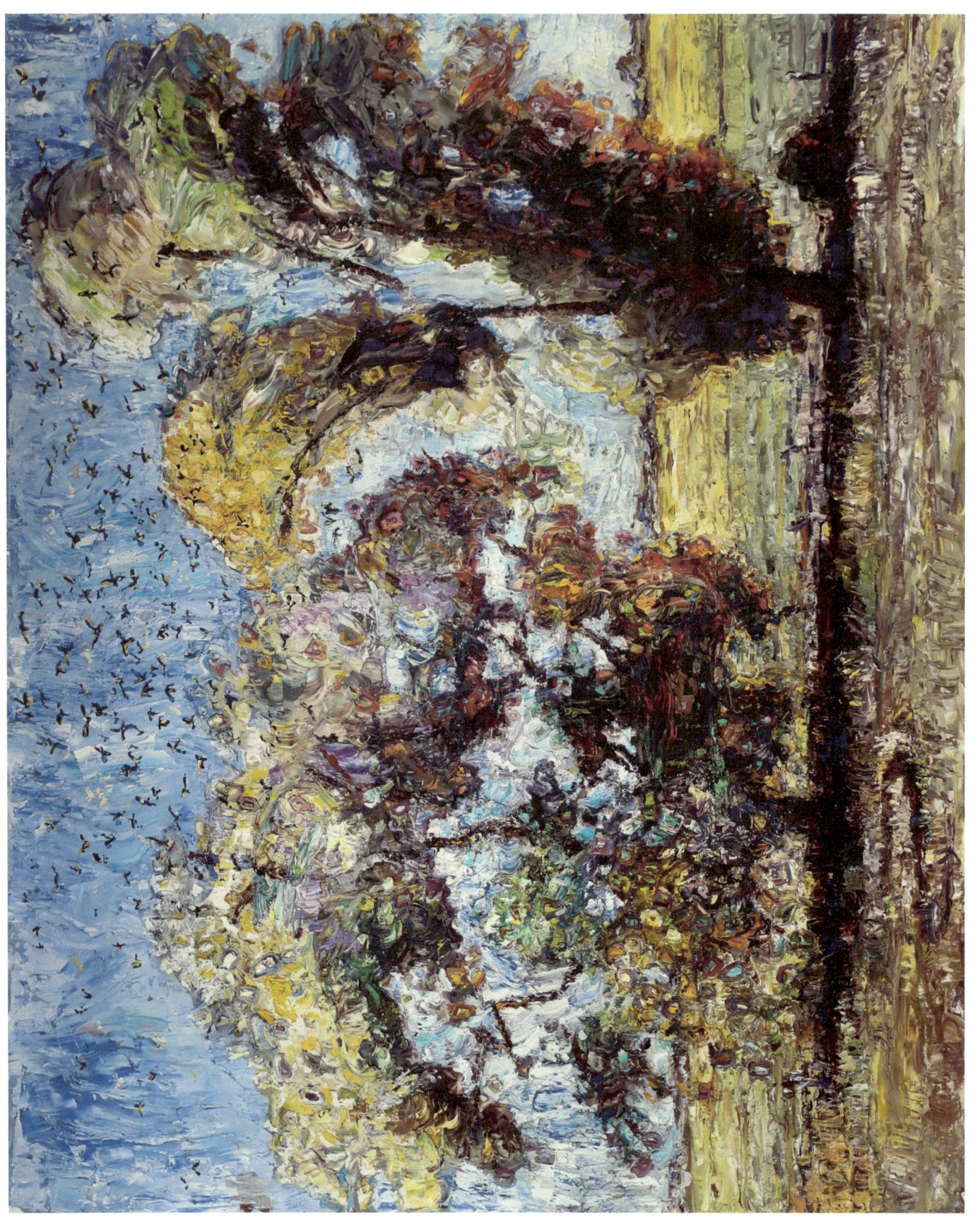

"Cottonwoods with Birds" 36" x 28" oil on Arches

"5 Flags, Taos" 48" x 36" oil on Arches

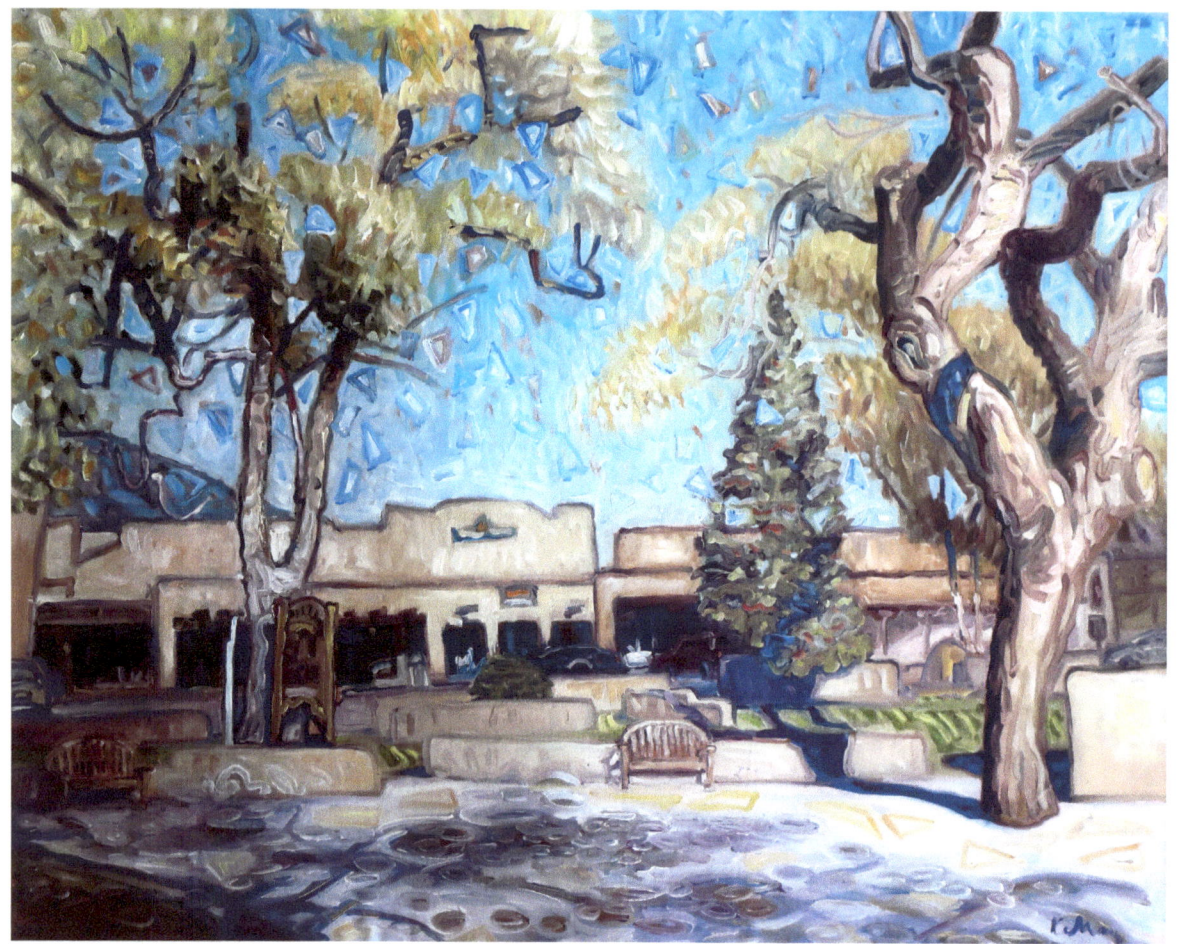
"Taos Plaza #1"   36" x 28"   oil on canvas

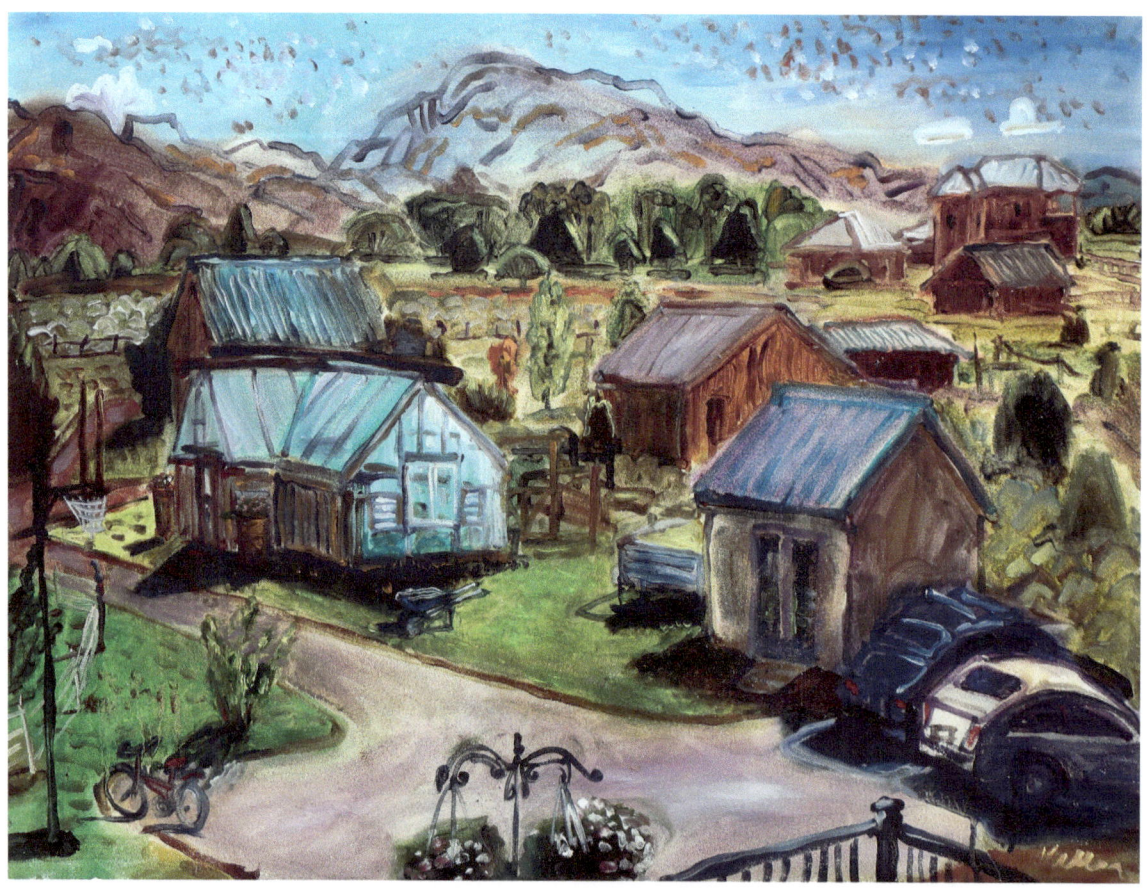
"View From the Porch, Taos"   30" x 24"   oil on Arches

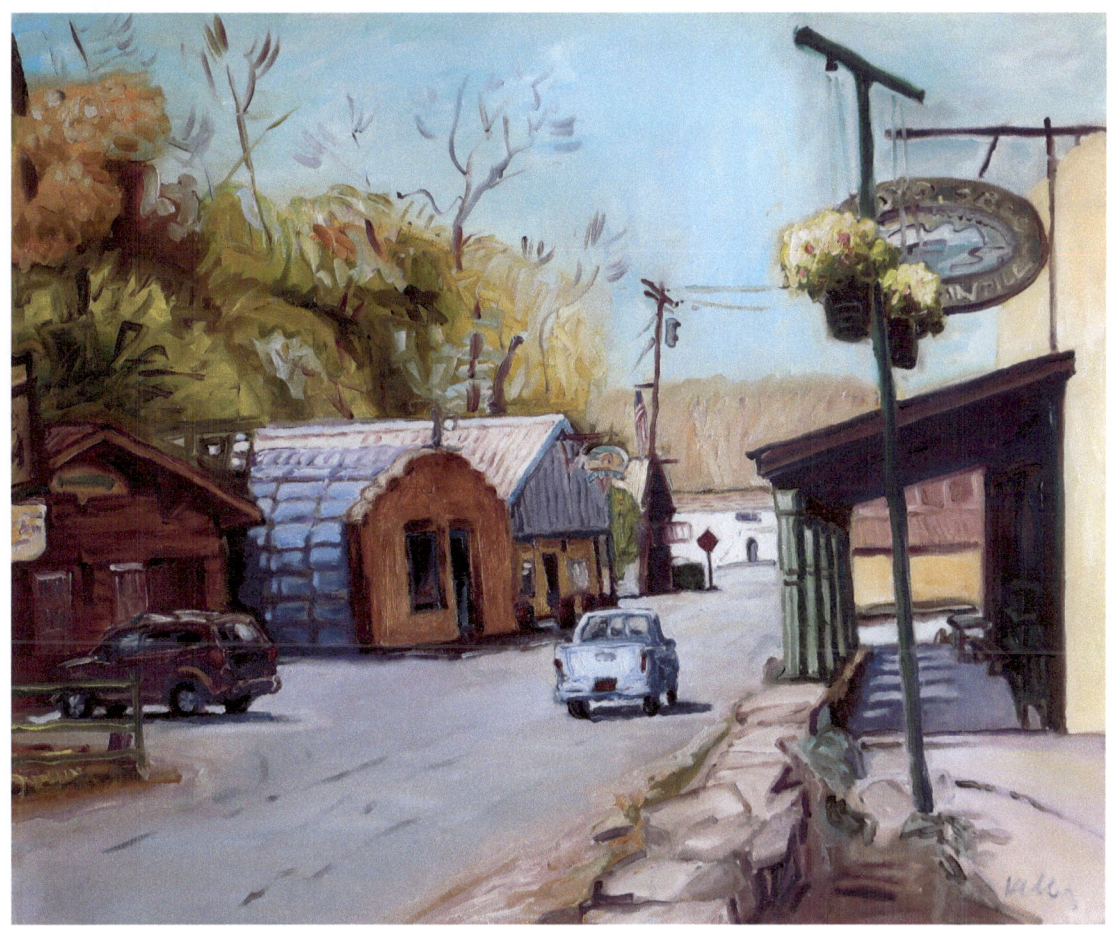

"Arroyo Seco Village"   30" x 24"   oil on Arches

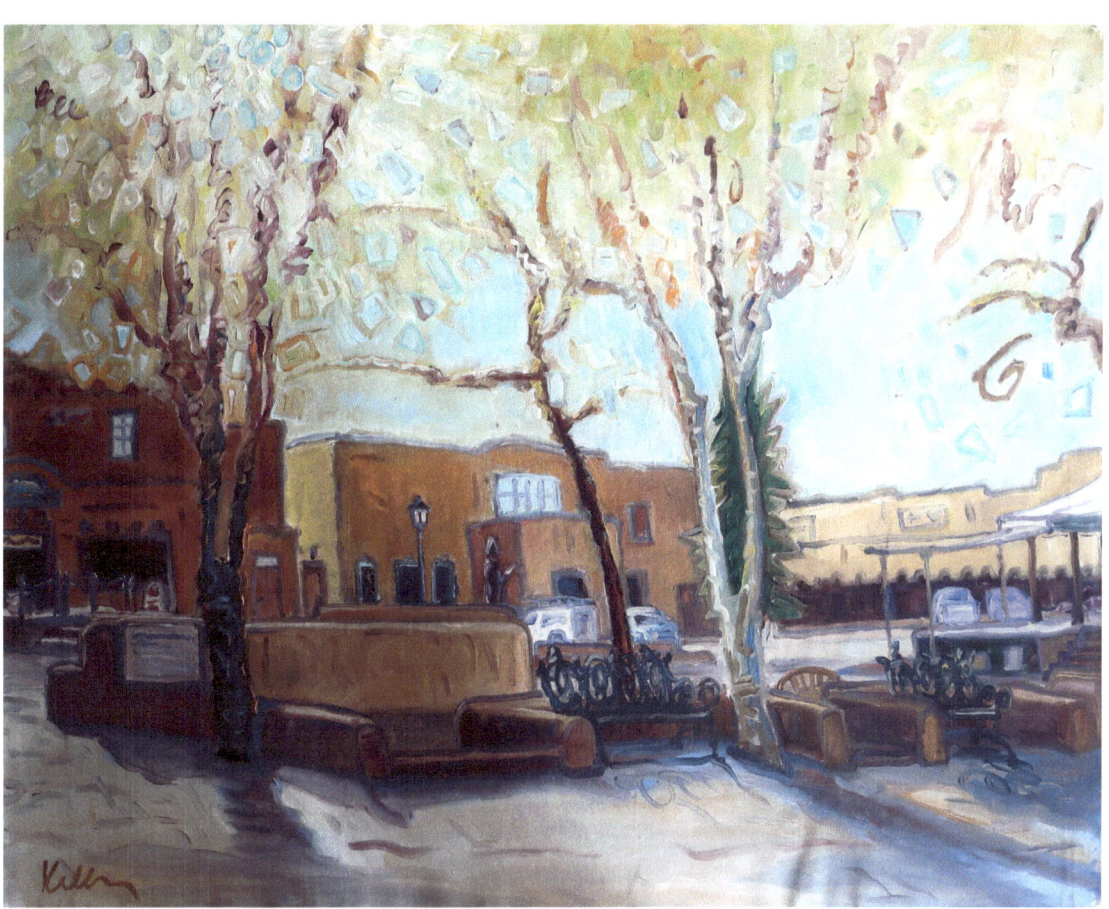

"Taos Plaza #2"   36" x 28"   oil on canvas

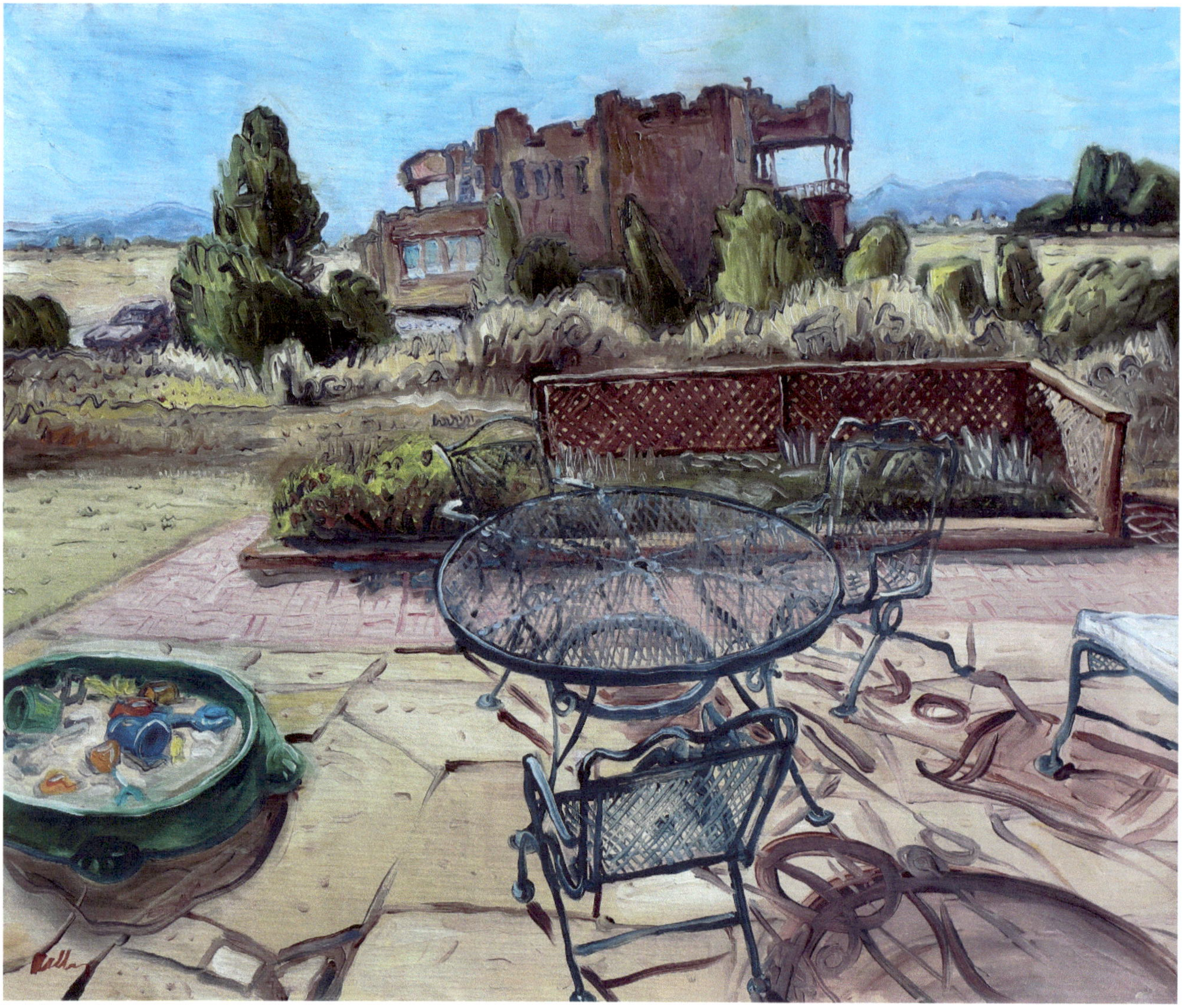

"Taos Patio #1"   30" x 25"   oil on canvas

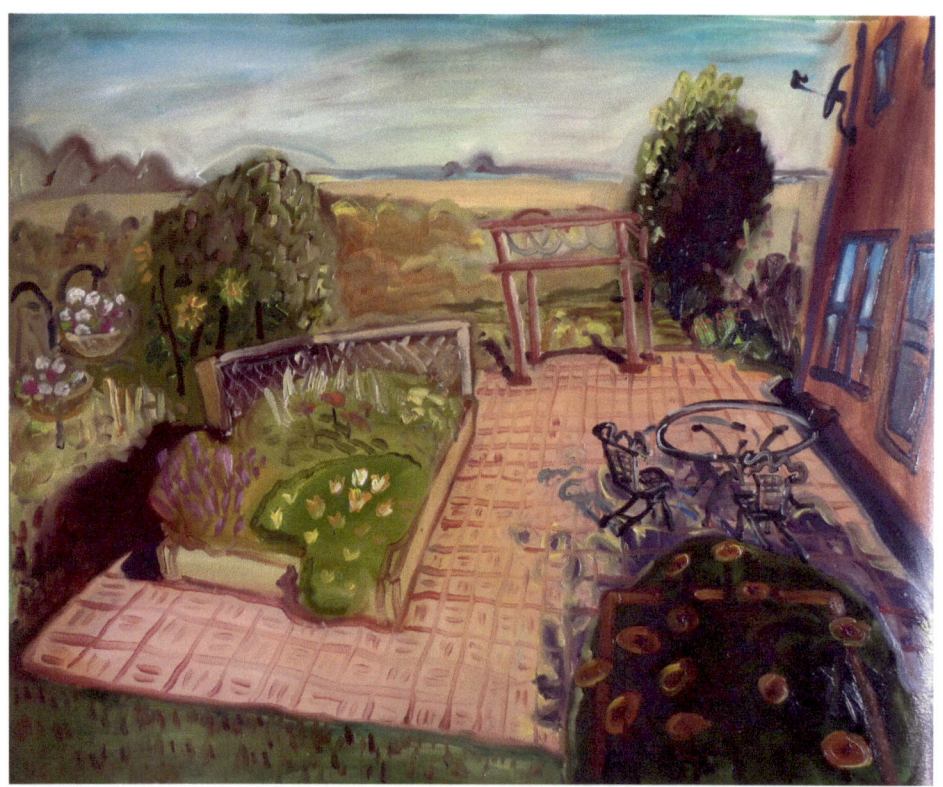

"Taos Patio #3"   30" x 24"   oil on Arches

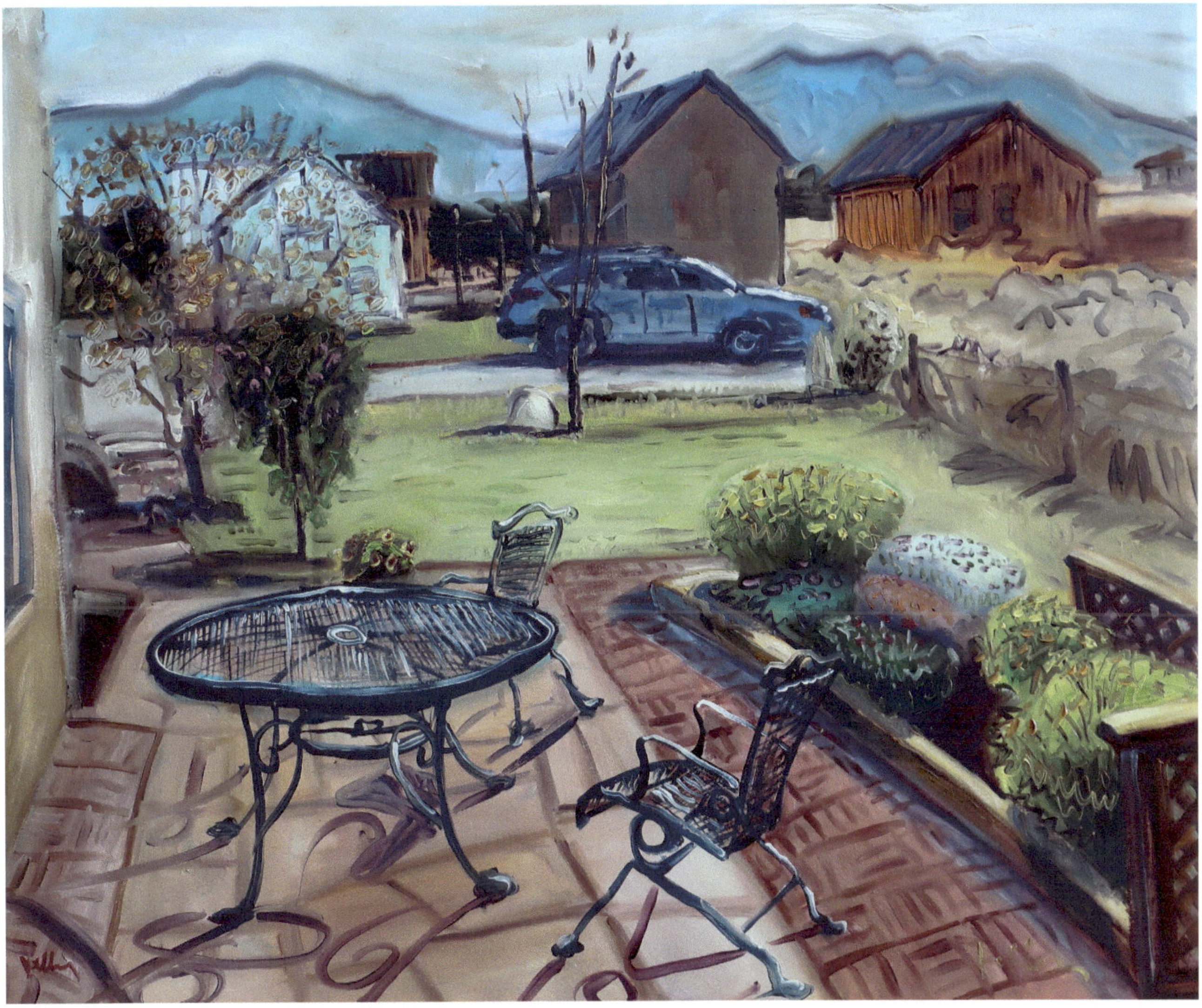

"Taos Patio #2"   30"x 25"   oil on Arches

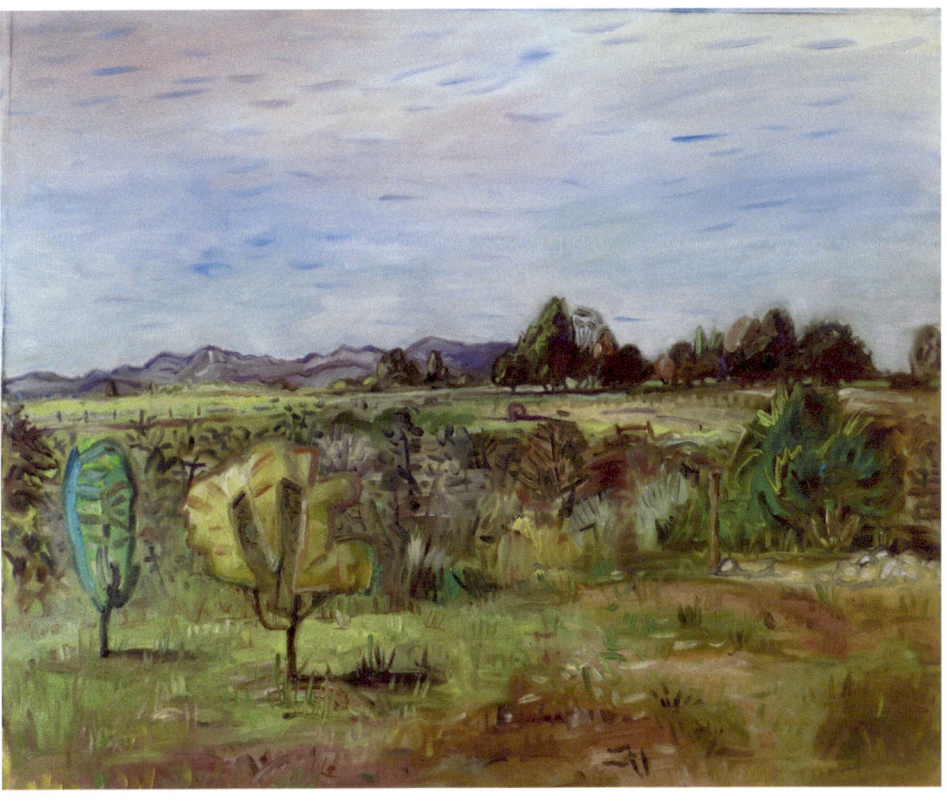

"Young Fruit Trees, Taos"   30" x 24"   oil on Arches

Watercolors

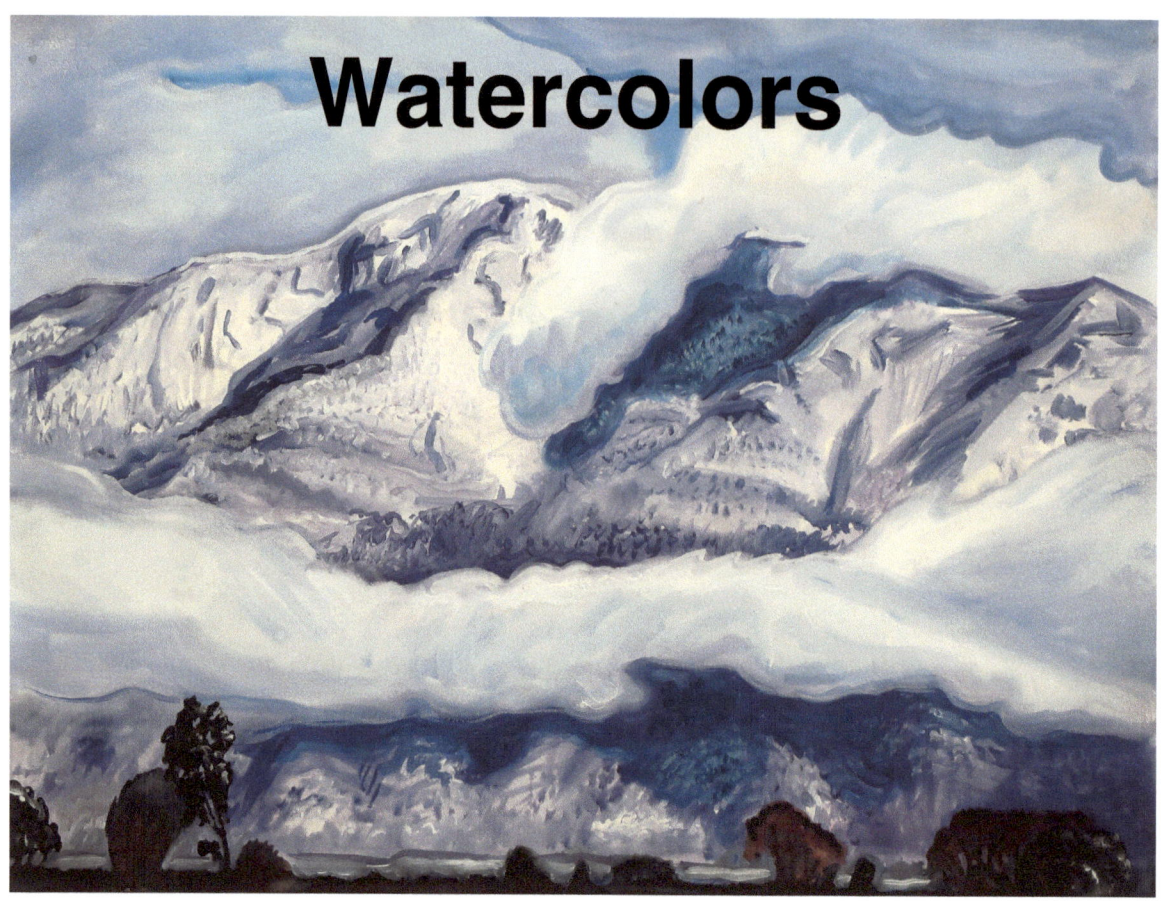

"Taos Mountain #1"   30" x 22"   watercolor on Arches

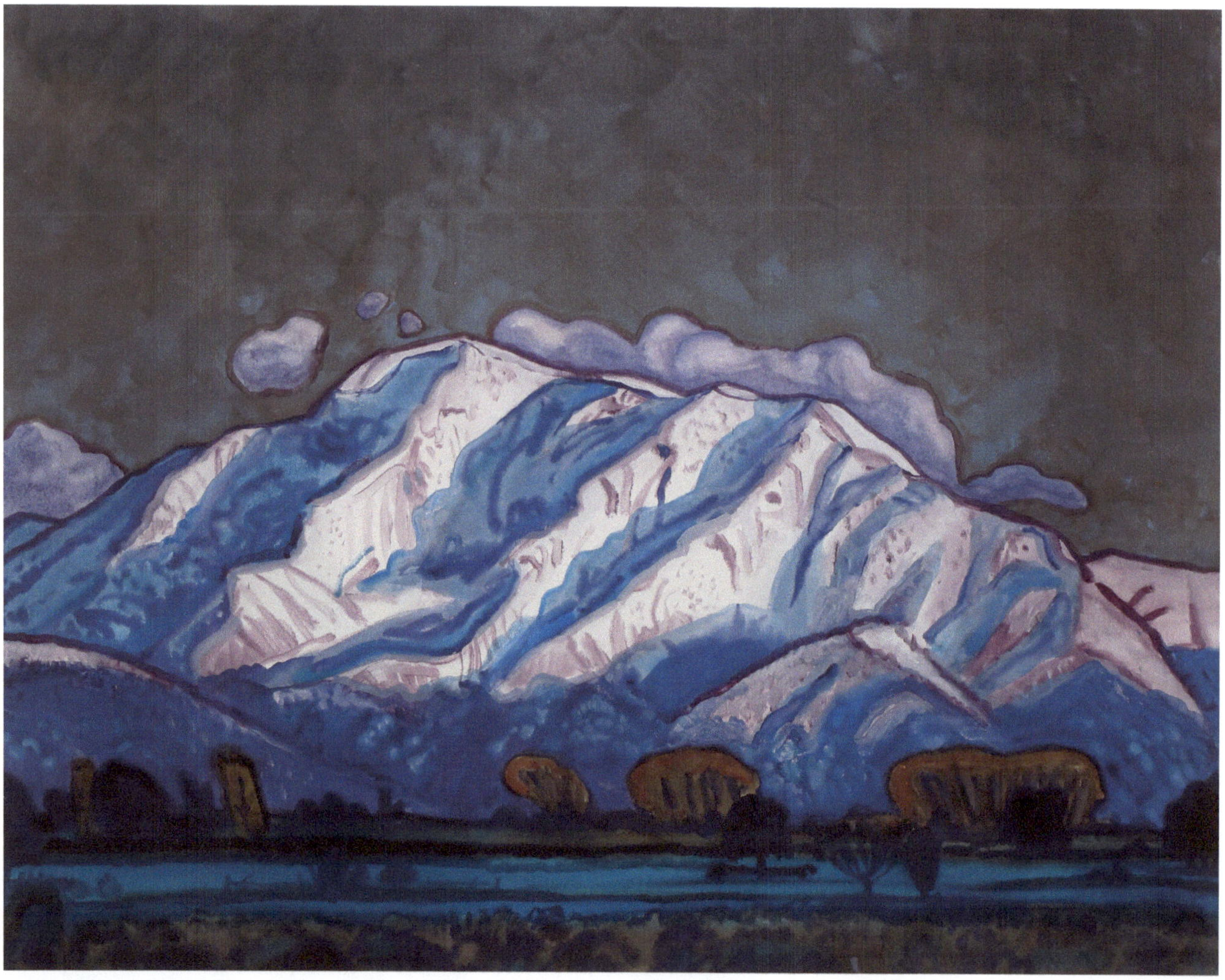

"Taos Mountain #2"   30" x 22"   watercolor on Arches

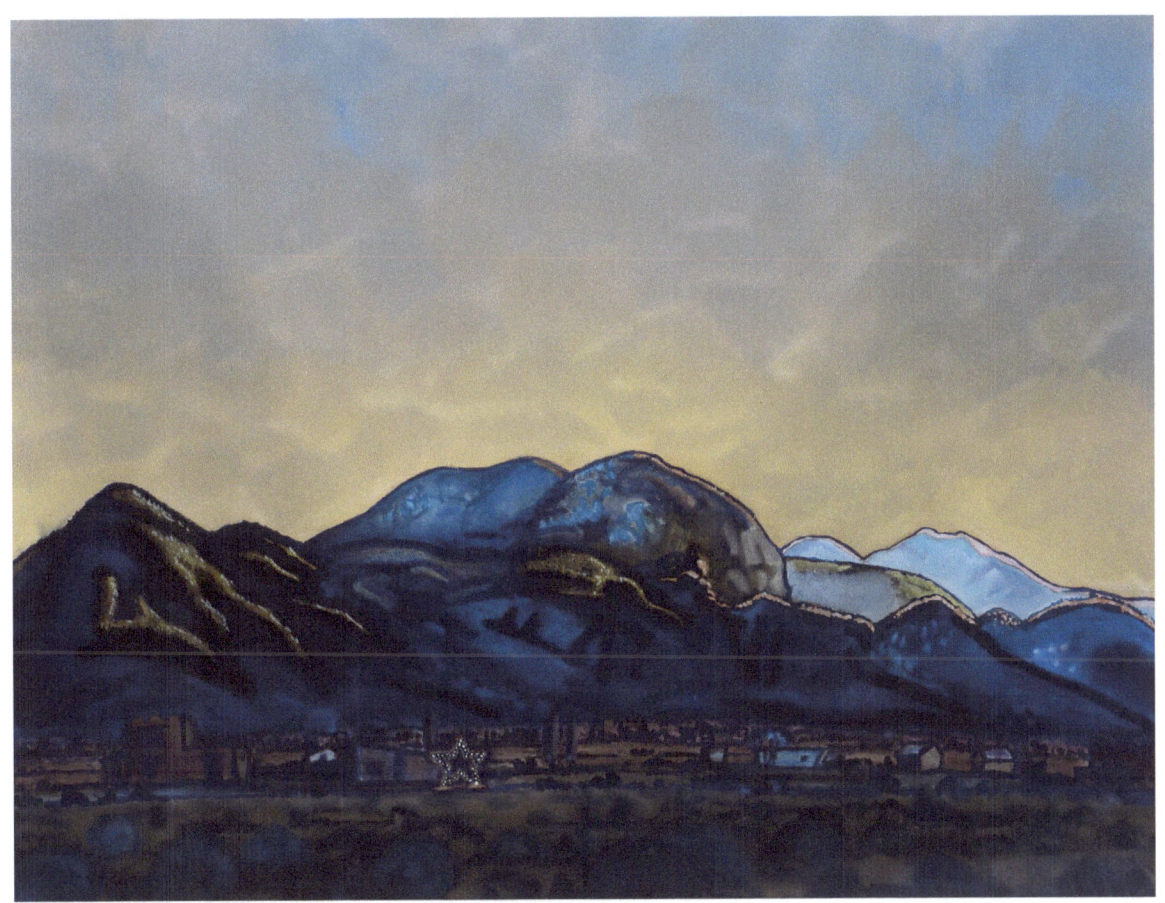

"Arroyo Seco"   30" x 22"   watercolor on Arches

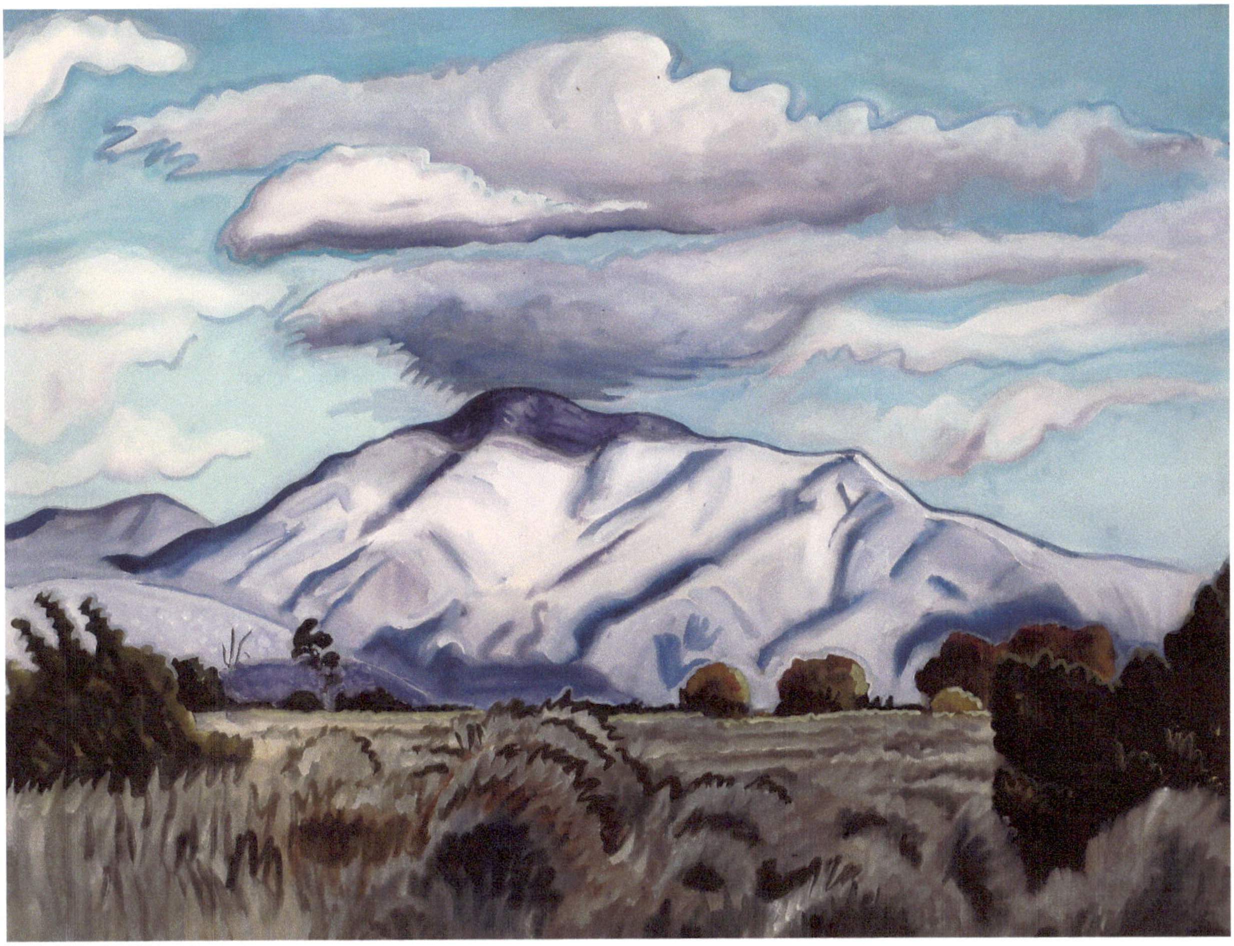

"Taos Mountain #3"   30" x 22"   watercolor on Arches

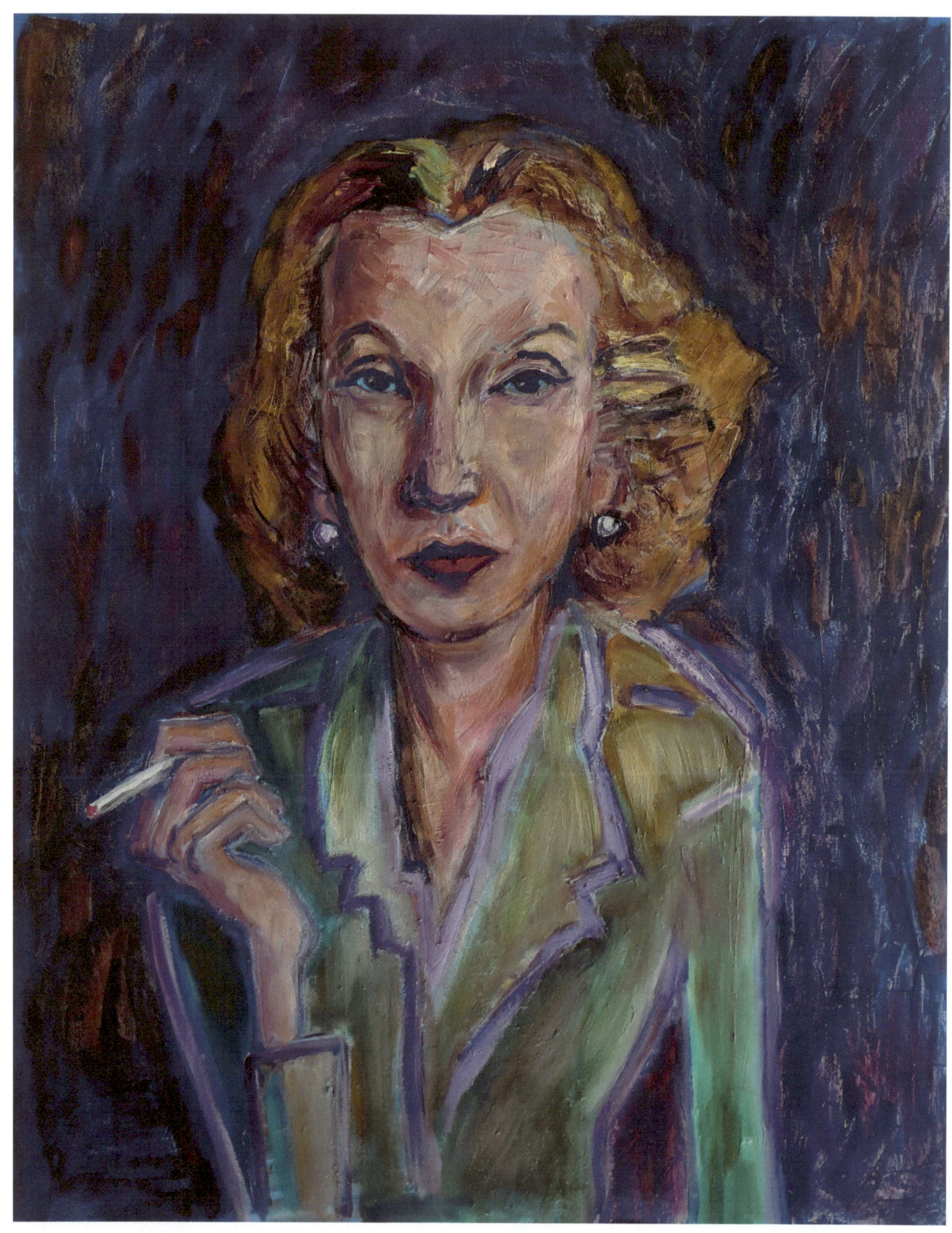

"Millicent Rogers, Taos"   30" x 24"   oil on Arches

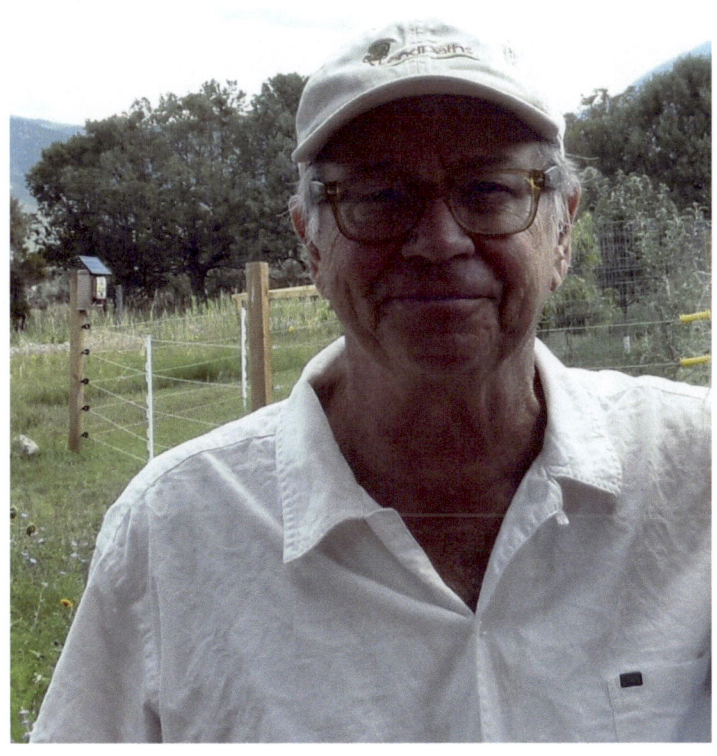

Ted Keller
40 Camino A Realidad
El Prado, New Mexico, 87529

tedkeller77@gmail.com

575 776 2705 - landline   575 613 3354 - cell

tkeller.artspan.com/home
(All of the Paintings can be seen on a full screen at this web site.)

www.facebook.com/tedkeller.painter/

Book: *Watercolor: One Person's Teachings on Watercolor Painting and Becoming an Artist Along With a Gallery of His Work: For All Levels of Skill and Courage and Interest*
by *Ted Keller*

For sale on Amazon, or directly from Ted.

www.ingramcontent.com/pod-product-compliance
Lightning Source LLC
Chambersburg PA
CBHW041934240526
45473CB00034B/1649